THE ARTIST'S MODEL

FRANCES BORZELLO

The Artist's Model

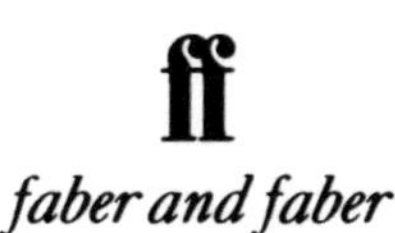

faber and faber

This edition first published in 2010
by Faber and Faber Ltd
Bloomsbury House, 74–77 Great Russell Street
London WC1B 3DA

Printed by Books on Demand GmbH, Norderstedt

A CIP record for this book is available from the British Library

ISBN 978–0–571–26982–2

Illustrations

The illustrations were reproduced courtesy of the following:

figs. 1 and 6, The National Portrait Gallery, London
figs. 4, 10, 11, 12, 13, 14, 15, 16, 17, The British Library, London
figs. 5 and 21, The Royal Academy of Arts, London
fig. 8, Anthony d'Offay, London
fig. 9, Birmingham Museums and Art Gallery
fig. 18, Honolulu Academy of Arts, Gift of Friends of the Academy, 1947
fig. 19, Musée Jacquemart-André, Paris
fig. 20, Municipal Museum of Modern Art, Dublin
fig. 22, Louvre, Paris
figs. 23 and 24, Musée d'Orsay, Galerie du Jeu du Paume, Paris
fig. 25, Kunsthalle Hamburg
fig. 26, Allan Frumkin Gallery, New York
fig. 27, Barnes Foundation, Merion, Pa.

Our authorised representative in the EU for product safety is
Easy Access System Europe, Mustamäe tee 50, 10621 Tallinn, Estonia
gpsr.requests@easproject.com

Contents

For R.A.B.

1
Fact and Fantasy

To admit to writing about artists' models is to set off an avalanche of interest. 'Didn't Rossetti marry his model?' 'Didn't Augustus John sleep with all of his?' At first I brushed such questions aside as frivolous. Instead of revealing the facts about modelling in England from the foundation of the Royal Academy to the present day, the gossip column approach to art history seemed to veil them. But as research revealed the mundane business of a model's life, I had second thoughts about my high-minded approach. I became fascinated by the way that contrary to the facts that were emerging, the majority of model anecdotes shared a common obsession — sex — and a common assumption — that models are female. I started to wonder how posing for artists, a tiring, tedious and lowly-paid profession practised by both sexes and all ages, could have become so fascinating to the public mind and also so distorted.

The fantasies about models divide into two: the model as the artist's sexual partner and the model as the artist's inspiration. More often than not, the sexual and inspirational roles are entwined. Fantasies focusing on the model's sexual aspect deal with her beauty, her sexual generosity towards the artist and her scorn of conventional morality. Inspirational fantasies show models benefiting from the heights they have helped the artists reach through the possession of eternal life via their painted or sculpted representations, in their privileged view of the mysteries of artistic creation and in the comfortable old age they inherit along with a priceless collection of works of art.

The same names turn up again and again. Phryne who inspired Praxiteles, Goya and the Duchess of Alba, Raphael and his mistress, Rubens and his young second wife Helena Fourment. In England the Pre-Raphaelite painters are magnets for model stories and so is Augustus John, although few people under fifty could put a painting to the name of this man whose sexual reputation has outlived his artistic one.

Most stories about models are connected with painters of women, usually, though not always, naked women. Yet a look round any art gallery or a leaf through any art book shows that sculpted and painted people come in two sexes and in a variety of costumes, shapes, sizes and ages. Most of these people are engaged in some activity or other; it is the rare person who is lying down and looking languorously out at the spectator. Clearly the female nude model accounts for only a tiny proportion of the model-based art that has been produced through the centuries. How could she have come to stand for it all?

The job of artist's model has not changed in hundreds of years. While nowadays the artists they model for take their paints from tubes and their pastels from tins, the models — male as well as female, old as well as young, fat as well as thin — arrive as they always have done, ten minutes in advance of their sitting, strip off or dress up, depending on whether they are to pose in the nude or not, and take up their position. If they are modelling for a class, they arrange themselves on the same sort of 'throne' pictured by Rembrandt in c. 1639 (fig. 1) and stay put for the same two hours with fifteen-minute break as was marked by the Royal Academy Schools' hourglass until its replacement by a clock in 1865. If they are modelling in a private studio there is likely to be greater flexibility of poses and posing time but even so, whether the model is an amateur or a professional, working in an art school for twenty students or in a private studio for a single artist, the model's role of posing to enable students to sharpen their skills or professionals to produce a finished work remains the same as it has always done.

It is not on the whole exciting work, though it has its compensations. Some models find it satisfying to be stared at. Others find the studio atmosphere so congenial that it compensates for poor pay. A few are flattered by the notion of sharing in the creative process, finding a reward in knowing that it is their presence and theirs alone that encourages the artist to produce good work. But the inspirational role is a rare one, and the reality of the job is sitting without fidgeting for great spreads of time at an hourly rate of pay that compares with waiting on tables.

The fact that they are paid means models become objects to be used as the buyer desires, and what the buyer desires is someone to stay still in the required pose for the required time. Models are part of another's learning or creative process. Although they are human, they tend to be treated like superior lay figures, the life-size jointed dolls that substitute when live models are not available. Although they are necessary, in the scrutiny they undergo they are in an odd way ignored. Since speech might interrupt their pose and the artist's concentration, it is not unusual for models to remain silent for the whole of the session.

It might be these features of silence and stillness, and also privacy — much is made in a certain sort of literature of doors being locked while painting sessions are in progress — that have made models objects of curiosity and encouraged the fantasies that swirl about them. What is certain is that in the transition from fact to fantasy, the mundane work of modelling has been transformed into a profession of bohemian gaiety and glamour. And the reality of ordinary-bodied men and women posing for poor pay in a local art college has been lost in a mass of notions about models as mistresses, models as inspiration and models as naked and female.

Particularly models as naked and female. The *Oxford English Dictionary* defines model as 'A person, or, less frequently, a thing, that serves as the artist's pattern for a work of painting or sculpture, or for some portion of such a work; *spec.* a person whose profession it is to pose for artists and art-students.' But the fantasy has supplied a sort of extra-dictionary definition as 'female who models nude for artists'. This popular meaning has been universally adopted in this century. On 6 December 1980, 'Life Class', a television programme on Quentin Crisp's recollections of his modelling days at the Camberwell School of Art, was illustrated in the *Daily Mail's* television listings by a drawing of a nude female model. It is a tiny but typical example of the automatic transformation of modelling, even in the face of contrary evidence, into an exclusively female activity.

The view of models as female is based on the assumption that painting is a masculine and heterosexual activity. That this is not so has been made clear by recent books on women artists. There have always been women painters and sculptors: lots of them in the last hundred years but many as well in earlier periods.

Not even the entry of women into art schools in the second half of the nineteenth century made any difference to assumptions about the masculinity of art since the women went into male structures and adopted male values and practices. In nearly every male artist's self-portrait or portrait of a painter with a model in the last hundred years, the model on the dais is a naked female. Dame Laura Knight carries on the tradition in her self-portrait of 1913 (fig. 2).

In this century when art schools have increased their intake of female students until they equal if not outnumber the males, the traditional correspondence between the male sex act and the act of artistic creation has grown stronger than ever. Painting is seen as an extension of male sensuality. In Aldous Huxley's *Point Counterpoint* of 1928, the artist John Bidlake, whom initiates recognize as a portrait of the painter Augustus John, replies to those who reprove him for his way of life, 'Nobody can paint a nude who hasn't learned the human body by heart with his hands and lips and his own body. I take my art seriously. I'm unremitting in my preliminary studies.'[1] Huxley does not have to state that Bidlake is referring to the female nude; it is taken for granted that the lusty male artist is heterosexual and the nude he paints and the human body he paints it from, female. When Mervyn Levy writes in *The Artist and the Nude* that 'In modern times the best drawings of the nude have flowed from the bedroom; or even from the sofa. It is only necessary to find somewhere warm and private where you can pose your model',[2] we do not need to be told that 'you' is male and 'model' female. But just in case we miss the point, he adds that 'There should be the least possible tension between the artist and his subject. (For this reason it is easier to draw women after one has loved them. Most full-blooded painters would agree with this, I think.)'[3]

Though the proof that artists have always worked from male models exists in the drawings, paintings and sculptures they have produced, this evidence has been overlooked in the fascination with the female model. One of the strongest reasons for the prevailing view of the model as female is its apparent naturalness. The male artist-female model relationship is seen as the norm, and other relationships either deviations (female artist-male model), too dull to consider (male artist-male model) or too threatening to the image of the artist as sexual hero (homosexual artist-male model.)

That the naturalness of the male artist-female model relationship was established at a cost to the facts can be seen from the hysterical reaction when a suspicion that things might be otherwise rose up from the national subconscious. Although art schools managed to keep women from studying the male nude model until the end of the nineteenth century, there was nothing that could stop women from doing so in a private capacity — nothing, that is, provided they had guts enough to run the gauntlet of sexual innuendo. The rumours that Angelika Kauffmann drew from the male nude model when she was working in London in the 1760s and 1770s refused to die when she did in 1807; in 1828, John Thomas Smith, author of *Nollekens and His Times*, determined to find out if there was any truth to them:

> It having been asserted that Angelica Kauffmann studied from an exposed male living model, which Mr. Nollekens said he believed — I was determined to gain the best information on the subject, by going to Mr. Charles Cranmer, one of the original models of the Royal Academy, now living, in his eighty-second year, at No. 13, in Regent-street, Vauxhall-bridge; and he assured me, that he did frequently sit before Angelica Kauffmann at her house on the south side of Golden-square, but that he only exposed his arms, shoulders and legs, and that her father, who was also an artist and likewise an exhibitor at the Royal Academy, was always present. I have under my care, as Keeper of the Prints and Drawings in the British Museum, a most spirited study of hers, dated 1771, of a male

academy model, recumbent and half draped;[4]

Unlike what was felt to be the sexual straightforwardness of male artists working from female models, the reverse position aroused a horrified reaction as if nature were being gone against in some perverted way. The male artist-female model pairing was felt to be so natural that it effectively prevented the growth of any alternative fantasy that might have been expected to accompany the entry of women into art schools. Behind the cartoon in *Punch* (fig. 4), which appeared just as agitation by women to be admitted into art schools was getting under way, lies a massive male prejudice at the idea of the male model putting himself in a position with regard to women that his female counterpart had held for centuries.

In showing that male artist-female model pairing is only a partial truth about modelling I do not want to deny its existence. Although it would be ridiculous to suggest that sex in the studio is the outcome of every modelling session, a sexual element can and occasionally does come into sittings. Artists' freedom to choose the models whose looks they like (unlike students in art schools who have little say in who sits on the dias) can set up an exciting atmosphere of attraction and flattery, and men as well as women who model today say that sex is not an unknown outcome of posing in an artist's studio.

Nor would I deny that models have played a crucial role in inspiring painters to produce outstanding works of art. From the classical historians onwards there are tales of male artists in love with their models or fascinated by their beauty and encouraged by this to reproduce their looks in whatever medium they favoured. Elizabeth Siddall and Jane Burden were inspirations to Rossetti in the third quarter of the nineteenth century. Their faces imposed themselves on painting after painting and the red-haired, ginger-eyelashed Lizzie and the switchback-lipped and dark-haired Jane became the two female icons of the age, figureheads of the Victorian war between the red and dark-haired types of beauty which were admired so much. Their stories have become part of the national art folklore: Lizzie discovered selling in a shop, setting up home with Rossetti, being loaned out to model for other members of the Pre-Raphaelite circle, marrying Rossetti in 1860 and dying in circumstances that, as Tim Hilton put it in *The Pre-Raphaelites*, 'felt like suicide';[5] Jane the wife of William Morris, no longer romantically in love with him nor he with her, worshipped by the drink and drug-ridden Rossetti in the 1860s.

My quarrel with the tales is that their picture of models as beautiful females whose role is to inspire and sexually serve the artist is so pervasive, fascinating and easy to swallow that it has succeeded in obscuring the facts. Such stories take no account of artist-model relationships that are not of the inspirational or sexual kind.

The love affair between the French sculptor Rodin and the English painter Gwen John, who modelled for his unfinished memorial to Whistler, has been examined with great interest. It fits the fantasy so beautifully: painter overcome with lust at the sight of his new model's naked body instigates an affair, thereby earning Gwen John a place in model history. But what is less frequently pointed out is that Gwen John modelled for other artists too, female ones, after experiencing a couple of distressing incidents at the hands of the male variety. Posing for artists was how Gwen John supported herself in Paris in the years before the First World War, and the picture which emerges from this, her occupation for several years and the source of her income before the collector James Quinn made her an allowance, is not so familiar or so glamorous. As well as detailing the affair with Rodin, Susan Chitty in her biography of Gwen John lets drop information about modelling which does not fit the exciting image at all. Mending stockings for women artists on a sketching holiday on which she is the permanent model, Gwen John feels her lack of status.[6] Finding food unappealing she grows thin and Rodin loses interest in her.[7] Desiring to be treated better she keeps it from her concierge *at Rodin's suggestion* that she is a model.[8] Left alone in a studio with a visitor, he strokes her naked body.[9] Dare one say it? Might there be circumstances under which modelling might be degrading?

The Public's First Law of Modelling is that a model's interest grows in proportion to her intimacy with a well-known artist. Because of this a lot of attention has been given to Edward Burne-Jones's passionate love for the beautiful and wealthy Greek Mary Zambaco at the end of the 1860s, and trouble has been taken to identify her in his paintings and drawings. But also because of this, much less attention has been paid to the woman model he employed most often, an Italian called Antonia Caiva with whom he was *not* in love and whose nude body he used as a basis for many of his paintings, even when the faces were drawn from friends and family.

The reason is that Antonia was a professional model from the working classes — a model, that is, who posed at so much an hour for her living. Though she was necessary to Burne-Jones there was no glamour surrounding the relationship. He used her as long as she worked well but when she wore out he lost interest. In her biography *Edward Burn-Jones* (1975) Penelope Fitzgerald says that one day the artist received 'an ill-spelt, ill-written letter' from Antonia in hospital saying 'Sir I was always obedient to you. I am poor and ill.'[10] What was the Victorian artist's attitude to the professional model he relied on? What was the professional model's status in the eyes of society? Fascination with the notorious aspects of the artist-model relationship has ensured that such mundane facts have never been discussed.

The distinction between professional and non-professional models is rarely made because it is difficult to be dogmatic about the dividing line. Artists have frequently relied on models who were professionals in everything but name. Lizzie Siddal was a model, even though Rossetti did not pay her by the hour (at least, probably not after the first few sittings)[11], but she was not for that reason a professional model, earning her daily bread by posing.

Artists have always reserved the right to take their models from all over the place, as a survey of Whistler's sitters makes clear. As a backbone there were the two successive mistress-models, the beautiful Irish redhead Joanna Hiffernan in the 1860s and the less known American Maud Franklin who stayed with Whistler from the 1870s until his marriage in 1888. In addition, there was the pretty girl glimpsed in the street; friends and family; the rich who paid to have their portraits painted; the performers in the music-halls; and the professional models like the three Pettigrew sisters who were brought to London on the brink of adolescence and posed for half a guinea a day. In her memoirs Rose remembers Whistler offering less and Hetty saying with a sneer, 'I'm so sorry, I'd quite forgotten you were one of the seven and sixpenny men.'[12] It is satisfying to think of the waspish Whistler being stung.

Though there were vast differences in the status and situation of those who modelled, the biggest gap of all was between the professionals who posed for pay and the amateurs who included everybody else. These amateurs, whether they were women of the artist's class flattered at being asked to pose by a famous painter or adventuresses from the lower classes each hoping her face would be her fortune, expected — and sometimes got — more from modelling than a shilling an hour. To date it has been the amateurs who have had all the attention: the mistress-model who moved in with the artist like Lizzie Siddall or Joanna Hiffernan; the best friend's beautiful wife like Jane Morris; the loveliest girls in the artist's milieu like the ones picked out from the Slade School of Art by Augustus John. I am more interested in the models who posed for a living, the men as well as the women.

Professional models have rarely spoken in their own voice and observers have rarely spoken with sense and sympathy on their behalf. By assuming that the fortunes of models are tied to the artistic theories of their time, it is possible to give an account of modelling in England over the last two hundred years. An examination of modelling through its relationship to the prevailing artistic ideas reveals how restricted the popular view of the model-mistress is. Set in its context, the picture of modelling which emerges is less glamorous than we are used to but more varied.

Notes

1   Aldous Huxley, *Point Counterpoint*, 1928 (Panther, 1978), ch. 2.
2   Mervyn Levy, ed., *The Artist and the Nude* (Corgi, 1970), p. 21.
3   Ibid., p. 22.
4   John Thomas Smith, *Nollekens and His Times* (2 vols., London, 1828), vol. 1, p. 69.

5   Timothy Hilton, *The Pre-Raphaelites* (Thames and Hudson, 1970),
    p. 179.
6   Susan Chitty, *Gwen John* (Hodder and Stoughton, 1981), p. 115.
7   Ibid., p. 74.
8   Ibid., p. 77.
9   Ibid., p. 78.
10 Penelope Fitzgerald, *Edward Burne-Jones* (Michael Joseph, 1975),
    pp. 82-3.
11 Pamela G. Nunn, 'Ruskin's Patronage of Women Artists', *Woman's
    Art Journal*, vol. 2, no. 2, Fall 1981/Winter 1982, p. 10, refers to
    the fact that the critic John Ruskin gave Lizzie Siddal an annual
    allowance of £150 in return for drawings.
12 Mrs Warner (Rose Pettigrew), *Notes on Steer*, unpublished manu-
    script in the University Library, Glasgow.

2
The Rise and Fall of the Professional Model

The official history of modelling in England begins with the newly founded Royal Academy's first expenditure in 1768 on the hire of four male models. The unofficial history begins a century and a half earlier when artists with an anxious eye on the versatile immigrant painters began desiring to paint more ambitious pictures than the portraits which had previously contented them. The addition of the subject picture to the limited national repertoire of portraits, portraits and more portraits opened the way to the employment of models.

The use of models is related to the state of art. When art is a simple matter of portraits that answer the sitter's requirements of sharply delineated features and clothes, models have no role. The stiffness so typical of the native portraits of the sixteenth and seventeenth centuries suggests that artists worked from a lay figure once the sitter's likeness was taken. Certainly a lay figure would have been cheaper and less fidgety than a model wearing the sitter's clothes. When art becomes ambitious and the qualities that mark a good artist expand from the ability to paint a likeness to the mastery of anatomy, colour, composition and perspective, as they had done in Renaissance Italy and began increasingly to do in England from the start of the seventeenth century, then models begin to play a part in the production of a painting.

The development of English painting ambition was accompanied by theories of what constituted fine art. By the eighteenth century these had solidified into the aesthetic of the ideal. The life that was put into paintings had to be better — its values more absolute, people more beautiful, actions finer — than anything found outside the frame. The way this was achieved was by idealizing and generalizing. Beauty lay in a sort of norm of perfection, and individuality, idiosyncrasies and flaws were banished. It was an aesthetic that had descended to England from Greece via the Renaissance and it found an important eighteenth-century voice in Sir Joshua Reynolds's prize-day speeches to the students of the Royal Academy Schools:

> The poets, orators, and rhetoricians of antiquity, are continually enforcing this position; that all the arts receive their perfection from an ideal beauty superior to what is to be found in individual nature.[1]

The theory was that only by studying a lot of roses could a perfect rose be painted. The perfect rose was desirable because 'a mere copier of nature can never produce anything great; can never raise and enlarge the conceptions, or warm the heart of the spectator'.[2]

Schools where artists could learn to produce pictures in the new manner were started. John Thomas Smith in his biography of Nollekens mentions several schools around Covent Garden which can be seen as attempts to guide students and artists into this new concept of what constituted a 'good' work of art. Michael Moser was 'successively at the head of several drawing schools' before he became Keeper of the Royal Academy on its foundation at the end of 1768. Gravelot kept a drawing school on the south side of the Strand opposite Southampton Street. Ozias Humphrey was a student in Shipley's Drawing School in the Strand.[3]

There is no way of knowing how drawing was taught in these schools, though it probably involved copying from other drawings and perhaps drawing from casts, since first Italian and then French art theory had enshrined these practices as basic principles of art education. Smith refers to a drawing academy which possessed 'a tolerable good collection of plaster casts' and this may have been something it had in common with other schools. Occasionally private collections of casts were opened to students and artists. For a short time in 1758, the Duke of Richmond allowed copying from his gallery of casts at Whitehall with instruction from G.B. Cipriani and Joseph Wilton.

Though it cannot be assumed that drawing from the model was part of the curriculum in all the schools, it was offered in the ones which attracted the most ambitious artists of the day. The earliest record of the employment of models comes in connection with Sir Godfrey Kneller's Great Queen Street Academy opened in 1711, where amateurs and professionals alike paid a guinea towards upkeep and models. In 1720, according to Sidney Hutchison, Kneller's successor Sir James Thornhill was deposed.[4] The short-lived academy he set up at his Covent Garden House was revived in 1735 by his son-in-law, the artist William Hogarth, in Peter Court, St Martin's Lane. Since this was the most important place to study till the Royal Academy opened its doors at the beginning of 1769, models were offered. The other academy which resulted from Thornhill's deposition and which opened in St Martin's Lane under Louis Cheron and John Vanderbank also had models. In 1722, a newspaper notice announced its winter season 'for the improvement of painters and sculptors by drawing from the naked'. There were others, too. Smith says that a school where Michael Moser was Keeper had 'living models, both male and female, and often grouped two or three men as combatants; so that Mr. Flaxman, who sometimes placed the models in the Royal Academy, was not the first artist who introduced that mode of study'.[5]

There are several pictures of drawing schools from this period, among them a painting attributed to Hogarth and owned by the Royal Academy showing men drawing a nude male model (fig. 5) and an engraving published in 1771 by Simon Ravenet after a picture by John Hamilton Mortimer of a handsomely built male model posing for a small group of artists (fig. 3). They culminated in the best-known of them all, Zoffany's painting *Royal Academicians* of 1771-2 which shows the members of the brand new Academy surrounding a male model whose position is being set by an Academician while another prepares to pose (fig. 7).

The opening of the Royal Academy's Schools at the start of 1769 signalled the entry into England of the long and structured academic art training which had been formulated in the treatises of the fifteenth and sixteenth-century Italians, put into practice in the academies of Rome and Florence in the second half of the sixteenth century and exported to France in the seventeenth. Drawing was seen as the basis of the artist's skill and was achieved in a three-part process. In the Academy's teaching programme, the student progressed from drawing from casts to drawing from the live model; the first part of the process, drawing from drawings, was mastered before entering the Academy Schools. Entry into the life drawing class was therefore the pinnacle of training, mastery of life drawing the proof of professional skill. James Barry defined drawing prowess in a speech to the Academy Schools as the 'skilful delineation or drawing of the human body'.[6]

The opening of the Royal Academy Schools gave the model an official place in a teaching institution with royal patronage. With its first expense in December 1768, the hiring of four male models at a retaining fee of five shillings a week plus an additional shilling for each night's work, modelling could be said to exist as a profession. Once the Academy offered drawing from the model at set hours several times a week, a new type of model developed. Organized, in order to be booked in advance several days or weeks at a time; fine-bodied, to approach the perfection of the classical ideal embodied in the casts of the great Greek and Roman sculptures; skilled in holding a pose before a group of students; punctual, so as not to disrupt the timetable. In short, a professional.

Just as the Academy's foundation increased artists' status through their profession's connection with an institution with royal patronage, so the existence of the Academy Schools improved the position of models. To work there was the goal, only to be equalled by modelling privately for a respected Academician. In 1837, a French model called Fleurat who modelled for a week in the Life School, asked for — and got — a silver commemorative medal, which suggests the status attached to working there.[7]

The eighteenth point of the Academy's Instrument of Foundation offered models of different sex and character and by early 1769 the male monopoly was broken when two female models were hired in time for the opening of the Schools.

Pay in the Academy Schools was good. Women were paid more than men, very much more so at the start when they earned half a guinea a sitting, plus sixpence beer money, which the men got as well. The high pay may have been a sort of shame money at having to bare their bodies or an inducement to encourage a superior type of woman to model. There is evidence that female nude models in the eighteenth century came from the same circles as prostitutes. A story by Smith suggests that a madam's cut could come from modelling as well as prostitution:

> One May morning, during Mrs. Nollekens's absence from town, Mrs. Lobb, an elderly lady in a green calash, from the sign of the Fan in Dyot-street, St. Giles's was announced by Kit Finney, the mason's son, as wishing to see Mr. Nollekens. 'Tell her to come in,' said Nollekens, concluding that she had brought him a fresh subject for a model, just arrived from the country; but upon that lady's entering the studio, she vociferated before all his people, 'I am determined to expose you! I am, you little grub! ... I'll tell his worship Collins, in another place, what a scurvy way you behaved to young Bet Balmanno yesterday! Why the girl is hardly able to move a limb to-day. To think of keeping a young creature eight hours in that room, without a thread upon her, or a morsel of anything to eat or a drop to drink, and then to give her only 2/- to bring home! Neither Mr. Fuseli nor Mr. Tresham would have served me so.'[8]

It is inconceivable that models could have come from anywhere but the lowest classes. In a society where class position was so clearly marked, only the poor would find posing for payment an acceptable occupation. Satirizing the artificiality of the rich, Pope wrote in *Epistle II: To a Lady*,

> If Queensberry to strip there's no compelling
> 'Tis from a Handmaid we must take a Helen.

It was rumoured that when the future Lady Hamilton and mistress of Nelson arrived in London she posed in the nude for the Academy's life class. It seems a plausible course for a beautiful friendless and ambitious girl to take, a chance to be seen by those who could publicize her charms.

The Academy was unusual in being the only national school to allow women life models, a taboo which extended well into the next century in some countries. However, a comparison of the male models' steady employment pattern throughout the eighteenth and nineteenth centuries with the women's fluctuating pattern reveals the Academy's attacks of anxiety about employing them. A series of amendments in its Council Minutes, doubtless related to current trends in models or morality, resulted in the women working less frequently in the life class as well as more erratically. In August 1832 it was resolved that the female model work only one week in four; two months later William Etty, one of the few early Victorian painters of the female nude and a constant life class attender throughout his adult life, had this changed to one week in three; in December he asked for it to be changed to two weeks in four.[9]

One of the reasons for this unwillingness to endorse study from the female nude as wholeheartedly as from the male was fear of immorality. Regularizing the confrontation between naked female models and male students was a serious problem to the institutions which offered drawing and painting from life. (Since women were not admitted into the Academy's Schools until the 1860s and even then could not study from the nude, the reverse problem did not arise.) The Academy fought the curiosity and innuendo of the outsider and protected those in its charge by a system of rules and regulations designed to damp down the fires of passion. No outsiders except the royal family could enter the life class when a female model was sitting, and attendance was forbidden to students under twenty unless they were married. Students were expected to keep quiet during the sitting and students and models were not allowed to talk to each other. If the model's pose needed changing, it was the Academician in charge who saw to it, and not the student. Students drew lots for their seats.

By means of this life class etiquette, which was enforced until recently (a sculpture tutor thinks that if life drawing is reintroduced into the art school curriculum a new student-model code of behaviour will have to be developed) the presentation of the model as an individual was avoided. Even so, references in the Council Minutes suggest that the presence of the female model led to trouble, particularly in the eighteenth century which had a more boisterous approach to sex than the nineteenth. In 1771 a notice was pinned to the Academy's door on the Woman's Night to prevent the ineligible from attending. After becoming a student in 1772, Thomas Rowlandson was rebuked for attacking the female model with a pea shooter; it is an early instance of his interest in the female body which later took the form of drawings, some of them pornographic. In 1793 a 17 year old was disciplined for obtaining a ticket to the life class. Perhaps he pretended to be married.[10]

An even weightier reason for the lack of committment to the female nude model was that the Renaissance theorists had not said much about her in their writings. The Renaissance treatises, from which is derived a major part of what was taught in art schools until well into this century, all imply, if they do not state outright, that the nude body from which artists should practice, perfect and produce their drawings, is male.

The male body was felt to be indispensable on two counts. First, because the bones, muscles and tendons were more clearly marked in the male body and knowledge of anatomy was believed necessary for the best drawings. And secondly because the fixed Renaissance views of male and female qualities — men were active, women were passive — led logically to men being seen as suited to a wider range of poses.

When the Renaissance writers discuss models, it is always male models they have in mind. Alberti in *On Painting* writes

> Before dressing a man, we first draw him nude, then we enfold him in draperies. So in painting the nude we place first his bones and muscles which we then cover with flesh so that it is not difficult to understand where each muscle is beneath.[11]

Dürer in Book Three of his *Four Books of Human Proportion* writes that 'in order that we arrive at a good canon whereby to bring somewhat of beauty into our work, there unto it were best for you, it bethinks me, to take measurements from many living men.'[12] There is no use pleading that Alberti uses the word 'man' generically or that Dürer plainly painted from live women in *The Hausfrau*, *Women's Bath* and *Three Witches*. The fact is that these treatises make no mention of drawing from the nude female model.

Leonardo da Vinci even denies us the chance of claiming 'man' is used generically. With him the model is always male since he specifies women, children and old people if these are whom he wishes to discuss. When Leonardo recommends the artist to 'go about, and constantly, as you go, observe, and consider the circumstances and behaviour of men in talking, quarrelling or laughing or fighting together',[13] the reader knows it is the male sex and not humanity in general he means because of his advice elsewhere to represent women 'in modest attitudes, their legs close together, their arms closely folded, their heads inclined and somewhat on one side'.[14] Holding such views, it is not likely Leonardo would see the nude female model as a fruitful source of action-packed poses.

Women did not even have the monopoly on beauty at this period. One has only to look at the magnificent bodies of the sixteenth and seventeenth century Saint Sebastians in the great galleries to understand that the nude male body was felt to be every bit as beautiful and seductive as that of the female.

Through the Academy's Council Minutes, one can watch the models ensconcing themselves with increasing comfort into the Schools. In 1823 the retiring room was cleaned, a carpet laid, and a lamp kept burning while the model posed. In 1829 two flannel dressing gowns were provided for the models. In 1838, a means of warming the model's dressing room was discussed.

Because in the life class the model had to sit for two hours without clothes, heating was a problem. If it was warm enough for the model, it was by definition too hot for the students. In 1829 a thermometer was provided to regulate the heat. William Etty's demand in 1847 for some way of carrying off the foul air and smoke from the Life School 'which under the present arrangement is most offensive and injurious to health'[15] was echoed by other people in other years and other schools. Israel Zangwill in his novel *The Master* (1895) mentions the big fire that was needed to keep the model from shivering on the throne at the fictional Grainger's and describes the muggy atmosphere that must often have developed in the overheated life class in the days before deodorants and no-smoking notices:

> Matt opened the door. A wave of insufferably hot air, reeking of tobacco, smote his face and his nostrils; a glare of light dazzled his eyes. He was vaguely aware of a great square room crowded with young men in uncouth straw hats, sitting or standing at work in their shirt-sleeves . . .[16]

Alongside the development of the life class went the development of life class paraphernalia. A throne to stand or sit on. Blocks for the heel to rest on while the model posed on the ball of the foot. Long sticks to place their hands on when reproducing the pose of a classical statue. Ropes to hold on to when the pose demanded the hands be held above the head. In 1837, the Keeper and Etty were asked to 'give directions for such apparatus as they may think necessary for setting the model in the Life Academy'.[17] In 1872 Leighton asked for an improvement to the background for the models. Many of these props can be glimpsed in the studio paintings produced by the Dutch in the seventeenth century and the French in the eighteenth and nineteenth centuries, and in the less elaborate paintings of life class models called *académies*. Today these blocks and sticks are hidden in the backs of cupboards, made obsolescent by the contemporary disdain for complicated poses. Only the throne goes on. William Roberts shows a female model, naked except for the red varnish on her toenails, sitting on a throne in *Posing the Model* of 1958 (fig. 8).

The admiration for great artists of the past meant that models who conformed to the images they produced were the most in demand. Most highly prized of all were those whose bodies resembled the classical sculptures which were felt to embody human beauty at its best. There were styles in modelling as well as in models. Models took up the poses of the classical sculptures, of Raphael, of Rubens. In January

1831 when it was Constable's month to oversee the Life School, he set the two male models in poses from Michelangelo's *Last Judgement* and the female model as Raphael's Eve. Eve required a Garden of Eden, which he organized, writing to C.R. Leslie 'my men were twice stopped coming from Hampstead with the green boughs by the police who thought (as was the case) they had robbed some gentleman's grounds'.[18] In March 1837 when his turn came round again, he wrote to Leslie that 'I have three men and one woman allotted to my share.'[19] The project this time was based on the poses in Titian's *Peter Martyr*, a work much admired by Turner as well.

For reasons of cost and complication, one model generally posed alone. Double or even triple posings were reserved for end of term treats. Typical subjects were a group of gladiators, the three graces and sometimes a picturesque contrast of dark and fair skinned men or women. Until recently, for reasons of propriety, male and female models were forbidden to pose together.

That the Academy demanded a well-developed body is clear from the Council Minutes of 8 June 1815. 'Samuel Dickenson Strowger, having offer'd himself to serve as assistant porter and model in the Academy, the Council proceeded to inspect him and resolved that his figure is not sufficiently good for that of a model.' He got £5 towards his travelling expenses from Portsmouth as a consolation prize. An entry in the Minutes for 29 November 1822, reveals the Academy willing to spend money on some artistic body building:

> Mons. Clias, Professor of Gymnastics from Berne, having offer'd to instruct one of the models of the Academy in various exercises for the purpose of developing his form — Resolved that M. Clias be engaged for that purpose at the rate of 50 guineas for 6 weeks, and requested to commence with Thos. Bromhead immediately.

A letter from C.R. Leslie to his sister in 1812 suggests that the same standards as prevailed in the Academy Schools extended to the artists' studios:

> I frequently see an old beggar, without legs, in Holborn, who was one of the rioters at the time Newgate was burnt, and had both his legs shot off by a chain-shot in that very street . . . I am told his body is remarkably fine, and that he has frequently sat to artists — very often to Mr. West.[20]

The bizarre quality of this anecdote extends to others connected with studio practice at this time. Nearly all John Thomas Smith's references to models in *Nollekens and His Times* have a colourful air about them. The hair of Nollekens's bust of Dr Johnson was modelled from 'the flowing locks of a sturdy Irish beggar . . . who refused to take a shilling, stating that he would have made more by begging'. 'Abandoned women . . . sat to him for his Venuses.' A legless Chelsea pensioner came 'swaggering on his buttocks' to have his shoulders moulded for the bust of Mr Perceval. The arm of a friend's daughter supplied 'an example of youthful round fleshiness'.[21]

As in the art schools the idealizing aesthetic lies behind the apparently random choice of models. Where the private studios differ from the schools is in their practice of taking the best from anyone — amateur or professional, social outcast or neighbour's daughter. Since perfection was the goal, perfection was accepted wherever it was found, even in the overdeveloped chest and shoulder muscles of a cripple.

Whereas artists working in their studios were free to pick and choose and indulge their idiosyncrasies, as they always have been and always will, those in charge of the art academies tried to regulate the appearance of their models. In the interests of discipline and fear of public reaction, the Academy authorities refused to touch the more outlandish models. The fact that the Academy models inspired Smith to so few anecdotes can be taken as a tribute to their self-effacing professionalism. They were merely the best-built specimens of humanity it was possible to find, reliable, still and able to adopt the poses of the great images of the past.

As the nineteenth century got into its stride, the aesthetic of realism began to take over from the aesthetic of idealization and generalization. The way in which the old view was beginning to shift at the start of the nineteenth century can be charted through two examples of C.R. Leslie's painting practice. In 1812 the young artist wrote to his sister

> I have considerably advanced with one of 'Hercules Reclin-
> ing on His Club' from the famous statue . . . I am copying
> it from a small cast . . . and have a living model to colour
> it from . . . I intend, in the next picture I paint, to follow
> Sir Joshua Reynolds' advice and take all my figures from
> Michael Angelo's works, altering some of them slightly.
> Sir J says that by this means you imperceptibly acquire
> a habit of thinking like him from whom you select your
> figures, and then when you come to introduce one of your
> own in the picture it will necessarily partake somewhat
> of the grandeur of others . . .[22]

By 1816, Leslie's biographer Tom Taylor shows that with
his Academy picture *Death of Rutland* newer ideas were
ousting this traditional approach: 'It was Leslie's first venture in his most congenial work — the illustration of our
English classics. Sir Edwin Landseer, then a curly headed
youngster . . . tells me that he sat for the pleading boy, with
a rope round his wrists.'[23]

Leslie's switch from Michelangelo's figures to the curly-
haired Landseer marks the new reliance on the model that
becomes so strong a feature of Victoria's reign. Behind it
lay a change in the aesthetic from a worship of the imaginary,
generalized and ideal to the worship of the realistic and
individual, a switch which in terms of art theory manifested
itself as a replacement of Reynolds by Ruskin. Reynolds's
exaltation of the perfect form, a synthesis of several less
perfect forms, was replaced by Ruskin's avowal that beauty
lay in nature's individuality.

Ruskin's writings codified something that could be seen in
Leslie's drawing of Landseer: the artistic religion of accuracy.
The Pre-Raphaelites painting every blossom on every bough,
Ruskin drawing ivy curling round a stump on Denmark Hill
with hallucinatory clarity, were examples of this religion
that saw a moral good in accurate representation. If God
expressed his goodness through the natural world then the
artist was performing an act of worship in reproducing that
world in all its detail. To read Ruskin on art is akin to reading
a sermon. Works of art are described as moral, pure or

expressive of God's purpose. His readers may not have swallowed it whole, but the godly overtones to his art criticism must have done much to fix the views of this great critic of the mid-Victorian decades in his readers' minds. Ruskin judged art by its likeness to life. With such an aesthetic principle established as tantamount to holy writ, school and studio doors opened wide to admit the model.

The aesthetic of realism had an enormous effect on the modelling profession, which in the second half of the nineteenth century flourished as never before or since. Artists took the principle of truth to life so literally that they were incapable of putting brush to canvas without a model before their eyes. Models became as necessary as paint itself.

With the artists' determination to achieve the photographic reproduction of reality which was the standard by which art was judged, modelling developed into a full-time profession. Harry Furniss's model Nellie worked a six-day week, giving two days each to Furniss, Albert Moore and Sir James Linton, the president of the Royal Institute of Painters in Watercolours.[24] It was possible to spend one's life as a model. From the artists' memoirs of the late nineteenth century come tales of models who posed first as children, then kept on throughout their lives, ending their careers as character models. Even though in their worship of accuracy painters would drag in non-professionals, the amateurs did not dent the professionals' work prospects.

No middle-class home could be without art in the Victorian age, and the varied needs of the painters working like machines to supply the expanding market in pictures meant that all kinds of models could find employment. Harry Furniss in *Some Victorian Women* wrote

> During this picture making boom of the seventies, many young artists, needless to say, started studios, and consequently those dependent upon art for a living, such as models, costume-sellers, and others connected with the profession became very active . . . Models were so greatly in demand at that time that one could not pick and choose . . .[25]

The increase in the number of art schools at the end of

the century, part of the national educational expansion, supplied an extra source of work. It is from this period that the Academy's star began to sink and that of the Slade, founded in 1871, to rise until by the 1890s it had become the country's most avant-garde art school. Many of the 62 'principal' schools listed in the 1895 edition of *Art Schools of London*[26] offered drawing from models, and besides these there were dozens of smaller operations, some concerned with training artists for 'black and white' work for the mushrooming illustrated journals, others no more than opportunities to draw from life. A network of provincial art schools grew up needing models to service it, but London remained the mecca because so many important artists lived there. It was to London that after her husband's death Mrs Joseph Pettigrew brought her three pretty daughters, Hetty 12, Lily 10 and Rose 8 in order to put them to work as models. Proof of her success can be seen in paintings by Millais, Whistler and Wilson Steer.

The entrance of women into art education after the mid century encouraged the opening of classes and schools where women could learn to draw from life safe from the presence of men. At the Academy Schools, the women followed a sort of Bowdlerized male course, forbidden to study from the nude and chaperoned by a housekeeper. At intervals they would petition to be allowed to draw from the nude. Their wish was granted in 1893 when they were presented with a male model wrapped first in bathing drawers, then in a nine-foot loin cloth, its length laid down in the bylaws, and then, in case of accidents, a belt on top of that. In a turn-of-the-century photograph of a Slade School exhibition, the women's work can be distinguished from the men's by the male models' lesser degree of nudity.

In the 1860s and 1870s when the Academy life class was closed to them, women who wanted to learn what the men learned had to make their own arrangements. Elizabeth Butler who entered the Academy in 1866 says in her autobiography, 'I joined a class in Bolsover Street for the study of the "undraped" female model, and worked very hard there on alternate days.'[27] A decade later Arthur Fish's biography of Henrietta Rae tells us that 'to supply the deficiency of the Academy School in respect to women students and the study from the undraped model, a proposal was made by Miss Margaret Dicksee to her fellow students that they should form a life class of their own on co-operative principles.'[28]

These young women must have been extraordinarily single-minded and ambitious. Where the male students had their course of art studies organized for them, the girls had to construct one for themselves. Elizabeth Butler recalls a 'big grenadier of a girl, who says she wants to know "all about the joints and muscles" and seems a "thorough-goer like my-self" '.[29] It is ironic that given the popular picture of the dedicated male student struggling against fearful odds to become an artist, the female art students had to cope with higher obstacles than the men ever did to achieve a similar education. And then when they got it, contemporary social attitudes and the structure of the art world saw that recognition and rewards such as high prices and membership of artistic institutions were kept for men.

All through the nineteenth century, the Academy Schools stuck to outdated theories and the advice in the lectures has an eighteenth-century ring. Sir Charles Lock Eastlake in his 1853 presidential discourse preached the superiority of imagination to students who in the previous two years had seen such realistic Pre-Raphaelite works as Holman Hunt's *The Hireling Shepherd* and Millais' *Ophelia* on the walls of the Academy's summer exhibition: 'An academy figure is therefore . . . essential to proper instruction in a school as it is, generally speaking unfit for the higher purposes of Art when the student proceeds to invent.'[30]

While the new aesthetic extended the model types the artists required, in the schools the clones of the great painted and sculpted images were still in demand. In *Manette Salomon*, the Goncourts' novel of mid-century Parisian artistic life, the art school models are categorized according to the works they resemble, and a similar typecasting existed here. Gilbert modelled for satyrs; Waill had the elegant legs of a sixteenth-century Italian drawing; Thomas l'Ours had the body of one of Michelangelo's Damned. Of the women, Julie Waill was built on classical lines; Madame Legois modelled for classical stomachs and legs; skinny Marie Poitou posed for saints, martyrs and mystics; Juliette had a Rubensian body.[31]

By the end of the nineteenth century, it was the turn of the mimetic aesthetic to be challenged. Iconoclastic views reaching from France destroyed likeness to life as an aesthetic standard by seeing the canvas as a two-dimensional surface to be covered in a pattern of forms and colour. The avant-garde found eighteenth-century notions of the ideal or nineteenth-century beliefs in photographic realism as irrelevant as drawing from casts. According to the new formulations, art was either a matter of form and colour which led to abstraction (proof that content no longer mattered) or it was a product of the individual vision which led to Stanley Spencer's nude portrait of himself and his pimply-nippled wife (proof that the notion of the ideal was finally dead).

The replacement of the aesthetic of realism by one of abstraction and/or self expression led to a fall in the models' fortunes, though the really dramatic drop did not come until after the Second World War and the triumph of abstraction. Even though artists in the interwar years were no longer involved like their Victorian predecessors in producing *tableaux vivants* in paint, they continued to work from the model, producing their personal vision from what they saw before their eyes.

In the art schools for the first forty years of the century, models continued to take up the classical poses. After the Second World War, the number of models in art schools declined gradually as drawing from life became discredited as the basis of learning to be an artist. The most radical change to date in teaching art took place in the late 1950s, when educational authorities brought art school teaching practices into line with an aesthetic that derided life drawing as a necessary component of artistic competence. Many who attended art school in the last two decades have never drawn a nude model. A few major schools, like the Slade, continued to believe in the importance of life drawing, but in most others it has been offered only if the students ask for it.

The decline of the model has meant that modelling, which supplied opportunities for full-time employment until the outbreak of the Second World War, has since the sixties become the preserve of the part-timer and the female part-timer, at that. The outnumbering of male by female models has several causes: the overwhelmingly female image modelling has acquired in this century; the fact that the majority of teachers of fine art are men (women tending to be employed in less prestigious departments like print-making or illustration) and do not wish to work from male models; the death of the Renaissance belief that skill depends on knowledge of the nude male body.

The flexibility which appeals to the part-timer is one of the reasons it lacks appeal as a career. A school or artist tends to hire models for a specific period but then, in the interests of variety, may not recall them for several months. Poor pay, around £2 an hour in the London schools, does not help, nor does the lack of a central agency that could save models the time and expense of contacting prospective employers.

Even more important is the lack of any definition of what being a good model entails. The paradox about modelling is that while it is regarded as unskilled work (proof being its poor pay and amateur practitioners) it is also, as all artists will tell you, a gift, and the 'good model' a fact. Artists constantly refer to this creature, although when asked to define it they have trouble. The ability to keep still and be punctual, a good figure, talent in finding poses and stamina in sustaining a painful position are some of the qualities put forward. There are stories of women waddling like sealions on to the dias then adopting a knowing pose which liberates the students' pencils through the lines of the body and the folds of the flesh. Sometimes artists come close to describing a good model by describing a bad. In the sixties at the Slade there was a craze for pregnant models, but their condition made them sleepy and a sleeping model was not acceptable.

Artists' inability to describe a good model would not matter if there were professionals around who could pass on the skills which make modelling a career. Few models today would take their work as seriously as Quentin Crisp in the Second World War when he did everything but hang from the ceiling in order to jolt the students out of their conventional ways of seeing.[32]

Because modelling has lost its professional aura, it tends to attract a mixed group of practitioners: au pairs, single mothers, art students, out-of-work artists. Probably none of them took up the work after surveying themselves in a full-length mirror and deciding modelling was the right career. Most of today's models go in for it because they are artists, or know artists or are art students or know someone who models. Because modelling has no professional structure, no union and therefore no official voice, it is only those with links with the art world who consider it.

Nowadays modelling for artists has lost its image. No careers officer would suggest artist's model as a job to a school leaver. The model's disappearance from contemporary consciousness in any realistic sense (though the image of the naughty artist's model lives on) is shown in the four-page entry under Model in Ruth Miller's *Equal Opportunities*.[33] Among its meanings of runway clothes model, photographic model and advertising model, there is no awareness that model might refer to artist's model, no suggestion that posing for artists might make a career. The meaning of model as a woman who models clothes has become so much the norm in the last forty years that any other type of model, like the artist's model or the male model, have to be identified as such.

As the modernist aesthetic which has stressed form and played down content loses favour, there are signs which suggest the situation may be on the turn. The art press talks of the 'New Realism'. There are noises from art schools of a desire to return to drawing from life, the art world's equivalent of educationalists' hankerings after the three Rs. Schools like the Slade which have clung to the figure are finding that their position of educational reactionary has changed to one of educational trendy. Attention is being paid to influential artists like David Hockney who have always believed in life drawing as a basis of skill and have always used their friends as models.

As the aesthetic has changed over the centuries, it has affected the numbers and types of models required. Their numbers increased in the eighteenth century, peaked in the second half of the nineteenth century and began to diminish after the Second World War. Far from being an occupation for females only, men have always worked as models, being joined in the nineteenth century by a whole casting agency of character models. Not till the middle of this century did women take over.

Of all the aesthetics, it was the nineteenth-century belief in likeness to life that boosted the model's importance. In the eighteenth century the model with the perfect body, or perfect bits of body, was the most prized, the one who could help the students and artists produce the improvement on nature which the aesthetic of idealization and generalization demanded. In this century the decline in the importance of meticulous copying from life has been matched by a decline in the number of models, although they still have a limited role to play in education and in the work of certain artists. In the second half of the nineteenth century the demands of the aesthetic for a meticulous copying of reality led to a peak on the graph of the models' importance. From about 1870 to the outbreak of the First World War was the golden age of the artist's model. As such it deserves a chapter to itself.

Notes

1 Sir Joshua Reynolds, *Discourses on Art*, ed. R. Wark (Huntington Library Publications, 1959), Discourse 3, p. 42.
2 Ibid., p. 41.
3 John Thomas Smith, *Nollekens and His Times* (2 vols., London, 1828): Moser, vol. 1, p. 60; Gravelot, vol. 2, p. 208; Shipley's, vol. 2, p. 358.
4 See Sidney C. Hutchison, 'The Royal Academy Schools', *Walpole Society* (Oxford), vol. 38, 1960-62, pp. 123-4 for a full account of information in this paragraph.
5 Smith, *Nollekens*, vol. 2, p. 230.
6 R. Wornum, ed., *Lectures on Painting by the Royal Academicians Barry, Opie and Fuseli* (London, 1848), James Barry, Lecture 3, 'On Design', p. 120.
7 H.C. Morgan, *A History of the Organisation and Growth of the Royal Academy Schools from the Beginning of the Academy to 1836 with Special Reference to Academic Teaching and Conditions of Study, 1768-1836* (unpublished PhD thesis, University of Leeds, 1964), part 2, 1837-1878 (Leeds, 1968), part 2, p. 21. All Council Minute references are taken from this source.
8 Smith, *Nollekens*, vol. 1, pp. 385-6.
9 Morgan, *Royal Academy Schools*, part 2, pp. 21-2.
10 Ibid.: Woman's Night, 1771, p. 50; Rowlandson, p. 51; 17 year old, part 1, p. 45.

11 Leon Battista Alberti, *On Painting* (Yale University Press, 1971), Book 2, p. 73.
12 Albrecht Dürer, *Four Books on Human Proportion*, quoted in E.G. Holt, *A Documentary History of Art* (Anchor, 1957) vol. 1, p. 324.
13 Jean Paul Richter, *The Literary Works of Leonardo da Vinci*, (2 vols., Oxford University Press, 1939), vol. 1, section 571.
14 Ibid., vol. 1, section 583.
15 Morgan, *Royal Academy Schools*, part 1, p. 53.
16 Israel Zangwill, *The Master* (London, 1895), p. 130.
17 Morgan, *Royal Academy Schools*, part 1, p. 53.
18 C.R. Leslie, *Memoirs of the Life of John Constable* (Phaidon, 1951), p. 188.
19 Peter Leslie, ed., *The Letters of John Constable* (London, 1931) p. 163.
20 Tom Taylor, ed., *Autobiographical Recollections by the Late Charles Robert Leslie, R.A.* (2 vols., London, 1860), vol. 2, pp. 12-13.
21 Smith, *Nollekens*: Dr Johnson, vol. 1, p. 52; Venuses, vol. 1, p. 111; Chelsea pensioner, vol. 1, pp. 409-10; friend's daughter, vol. 2, pp. 231-2.
22 Taylor, *Leslie*, vol. 2, pp. 14 and 17.
23 Ibid., vol. 2, p. 44.
24 Harry Furniss, *Some Victorian Women* (London, 1923), pp. 103-4.
25 Ibid., p. 100.
26 Tessa Mackenzie, ed., *The Art Schools of London, 1895* (Chapman and Hall, 1895).
27 Elizabeth Butler, *An Autobiography* (London, 1922), p. 46.
28 Arthur Fish, *Henrietta Rae* (London, 1905), p. 26.
29 Butler, *An Autobiography*, pp. 41-2.
30 Sir Charles Lock Eastlake, *Discourse Delivered to the Students of the Royal Academy on December 10, 1853* (London, 1854), p. 13.
31 Edmond and Jules de Goncourt, *Manette Salomon*, 1866 (Paris, 1896), ch. 8.
32 Quentin Crisp, *The Naked Civil Servant*, 1968 (Fontana, 1977), p. 131.
33 Ruth Miller, *Equal Opportunities, A Careers Guide* (Penguin, 1981), pp. 287-9.

3
The Heyday of the Professional Model

The late nineteenth century was the golden age of the artist's model. Their numbers started increasing around 1850 and their role in artistic life continued until the Second World War, but the period when the models had most work and most importance was from 1870 to 1914. Before that the production of the realistic story-telling canvases which typified the art of the second half of the century had not got into its stride. After that, disturbing French ideas about colour and form and personal vision seeped into the English art world and slowly killed off the artists' dependence on models.

Testimony to the existence of the professional model — always wistfully seen in terms of the past — can still be found today. There are those in art schools who recall there were one or two still working in the early sixties, 'tough old birds, not pretty, often middle-aged and with the power to stand for hours'. Quentin Crisp says in his autobiography that there were a few of what he calls 'devotees of the profession' around when he began to model in art schools in 1940.[1] A Slade staff member has memories of an old professional model in the 1940s who used to bring in his own axes and shields to introduce some variety into the poses it was left to him to invent in the final minutes of the class. Sir William Coldstream remembers whole families of Italians who made a career of modelling in the twenties. In the way each generation looks nostalgically back to a golden age of professional models one might be forgiven for suspecting it had never existed. But there is evidence that puts a stop to memories reaching ever further back in time.

On 27 January 1894, *Punch*, which still had an occasional

pricking of the social conscience which had been one of the reasons for its foundation in 1841, published a poem called 'The Ballad of the Professional Model' (fig. 10). It tells the tale of a poor and hungry old male model who looks into a gallery window and sees the painting of the prosperous patriarch he had modelled for, standing with food to hand and lavish clothes on his back on an oriental rug. If only, he thinks, I could change places with the painted version of myself. The ballad ends most pathetically

> Good-bye to you, old patriarch,
>   There in your frame of gold —
> The days are growing short and dark,
>   The nights are bitter cold.
>
> And the winds on the Embankment probe
>   One's life out as one lies;
> But I'll think of you in your robe,
>   Under those sunny skies.

This exercise in the manner, if not the meter, of Hood's 'Song of the Shirt', which had appeared in *Punch* half a century earlier, is proof that the professional artist's model existed as a recognized social type in the second half of the nineteenth century. In January 1889, in an article entitled 'London Models' in *The English Illustrated Magazine*, Oscar Wilde claimed that 'Professional models are a purely modern invention . . . the model, in our sense of the word, is the direct creation of Academic Schools.'

The most important aspect of the models' professionalism was felt to be punctuality. Because artists could not paint without the model before them, a model's late arrival meant a waste of precious working time. Many artists worked through the winter with the aim of completing their pictures for the Royal Academy summer show in May. Weak winter light and short days meant that to get the most from a working day models had to be dovetailed into the daylight hours. Punctuality or lack of it is a standard feature of many model descriptions. Arthur Ransome in *Bohemia in London* presents its lack as an endearing characteristic:

There is a tap on the door.

'Come in!' And a girl slips into the room, apologises for the thousandth time in her life for being so late, and proceeds to change her clothes for the costume that will make her the subject for his picture . . .[2]

Others do not share Ransome's tone of gaiety. William Powell Frith considered lateness a great sin in a model, only topped by models who left him in mid picture. A popular model spent a lot of time rushing to get to jobs on time. A day in the life of Italian model Luigi de Luca who had been brought to England by Leighton is described by Estella Canziani as 7-8.30 a.m. a private sitting for her; breakfast; a sitting till 1; lunch; sitting from 2-4 p.m.; tea; a sitting till 7 p.m.; plus an hour or so in the evening.[3]

Sobriety was demanded in the men. About the model Jim Bishop Horsley writes, 'Though an entire ignoramous, and with the devotion to beer common to the majority of his class, he was of an enquiring turn of mind, and used to put most posing questions during his sittings as a model.'[4] A devotion to beer may or may not have been common to the majority of his class, but as a failing it figures in many of the artists' stories about their models. W.P. Frith, painter of *Derby Day* and other crowded canvases, says that Brunskill was 'usually perfectly sober, because he knew well that one lapse from that conditon would put an end to his career as a Royal Academy model.' One night (the life school was held in the evening) he arrived both late and drunk.

His attitude was that of a sailor pushing a boat from the shore. He had a heavy oar, with which he thrust against an impediment meant to represent a rock . . . I was almost under the man, and had a very difficult piece of fore-shortening to contend with, and was doing my best to master it, when the model said:

'I can't do it. I ain't fit to do it. This 'ere thing what I hold ain't right. Nothing's right; so I wish you gentlemen good-night. There now!'

It was 'good-night' to us and 'good-bye' to Brunskill for he was never allowed to sit again.[5]

The models were expected to be able to hold a painful attitude for long periods without fidgeting or fainting. Elizabeth Butler, the nineteenth-century painter of military scenes, describes a model of her student days suffering under a heavy suit of armour: 'He was consequently allowed frequent rests, when down his trembling arm would clatter and the instrument of torture on his heated forehead came down with a great thump on the table.'[6] But even with frequent rests, the job was gruelling. W. Graham Robertson who posed for John Singer Sargent's 1895 Academy portrait in an overcoat with a dog by his side (Tate Gallery), gives the inside story:

> Being but an amateur model, I was easily entrapped into a trying pose, turning as if to walk away, with a general twist of the whole body and all the weight on one foot. Professional models will always try to poise the weight equally on both feet and will go to any lengths of duplicity to gain this end.
>
> I managed pretty well on the whole, but the sittings cleared up a point which had long puzzled me: why did models occasionally faint during a long pose without mentioning that they felt tired and wanted a rest? One day the answer came to me quite suddenly.
>
> I had been standing for over an hour and saw no reason why I should not go on for another hour, when I became aware of what seemed a cold wind blowing in my face accompanied by a curious 'going' at the knees.
>
> I tried to ask for a rest, but found that my lips were frozen stiff and refused to move. Hundreds of years passed — I suppose about twenty seconds.
>
> Sargent glanced at me.
>
> 'What a horrid light there is just now,' he remarked. 'A sort of green —' he looked more steadily. 'Why, it's *you*!' he cried, and seizing me by the collar, rushed me into the street, where he propped me up against the door post.[7]

There is a great deal of exasperation expressed by artists about their models in Victoria's reign, but even a cursory glance between their lines suggests that models needed to be equally tolerant. Estella Canziani says that her mother Louisa Starr, one of the Academy's first female students, used to feed and blow the nose of a model she had pose for her without resting for nine hours.[8]

Lack of temperament was important. Harry Furniss wrote of his model, 'Nellie was an ideal model, she seldom spoke: she was not endowed with much brain, but had sufficient intelligence to understand the pose you required, and, what is more, the sense to keep it.'[9]

The finest models were thought to be the Italians, their popularity and numbers increasing in company with the immigration patterns as the century drew to its close. Five of the models of her student days at the turn of the century named by Estella Canziani were Italian. Among the most enthusiastic supporters of the Italians were the artists Leighton, Burne-Jones, Poynter and Watts who as well as admiring the High Renaissance artists worked in a High Renaissance style, drawing figures nude before clothing them. Georgiana Burne-Jones recalls

> a splendid Italian one, Ciamelli by name, whose head with its bush of blue-black hair may be seen in the triptych *Adoration* as one of the Kings. He ground an organ in the streets and sang to it very finely out of his southern heart when he was not sitting, and sometimes brought it with him when he came to model.[10]

W. Graham Robertson gives an account of Walter Crane drawing a Venus from a nude Italian male because his wife disapproved of his drawing from a nude female. Leighton is reported to have said on seeing a Crane Venus 'But my dear fellow, that is not Aphrodite — that's Allessandro', Allessandro being a well-known male model.[11] London was a pale imitation of Paris in this respect, which was flooded with Italian models at this period. Many of them would leave Paris at harvest time for the town of Anticoli Corrado, known as the town of models, and the French artists would follow them, drawing them as they posed in the nude under the vines.[12] A nineteenth-century Paris model called Dubosc, author of the only model's autobiography I have found, has scathing words for the Italians, whom he saw as taking the livelihood from old-time professionals like himself. They were keen only to make money, he complained, and if they were women to marry an artist.[13]

Many reasons were given for the Italians' success. Foremost among them was their professionalism. Frith reported that 'the small army of London models finds many Italians in its ranks, and, as a rule, they are amongst the steadiest and most patient, both men and women'.[14] Burne-Jones found them conscientious in keeping engagements and the best sitters. 'Amongst the English there was no tradition of art,' wrote his wife, 'and the women with few exceptions seemed unable to understand that an artist's work was serious or that it could matter if they failed him at the last moment.'[15] Dr Angelo S. Rappoport, author of *Famous Artists and Their Models* thought they were the best because of the respectable and honourable status of the profession in Italy: 'a man or woman who makes a living in the service of art by sitting for the nude earns almost a title of glory'.[16] There was also their looks, an important element in an age in which the black-browed Mediterranean type vied with the sandy-lashed red-head as the favoured female colourings. The classicizing artists must have felt there was a direct link between the nude males drawn by the Italian painters of the High Renaissance and the Italian models they preferred. In his address at the opening of the Slade School of Art in 1871, Poynter promised his listeners that he would hire the very best Italian models. What he liked about them was their feet:

The feet are always a most terrible stumbling block for beginners (and even to the most advanced students), not only on account of deformities contracted from various causes, but of the swollen veins and the purple colour which would not be found in so great an extent in a person in motion but which naturally result from the model being obliged to stand for hours together in one position. It is true, that as far as I am able to manage it, you will be supplied with good Italian models to work from. These are not only in general build and proportion, and in natural grace and dignity far superior to our English models; but they have a natural beauty, especially in the extremities which no amount of hard labour seems to spoil. Their hands though many of them have been field labourers in their own country, might be envied by many of a better position amongst ourselves; while their feet, bare in infancy, are covered later in life by a natural and simple kind of sandal, which protects them without altering their shape, so that they do not run that risk of disfigurement, which is unavoidable with the hard and misshapen shoes and boots, in which the feet of children in this country are ruthlessly imprisoned, even before they are able to walk.[17]

In nineteenth-century terms this is not the singular obsession it might appear. For one thing it was shared by many. The model heroine of George Du Maurier's *Trilby* has beautiful feet. Despite the temptation to indulge in sexual or psycho-analytic interpretations, there was a perfectly good artistic reason for this interest in the extremities, that of the problem of reconciling art and life. Artists' ideas of perfection had been formed by the perfect feet of the classical sculptures and Poynter's speech suggests that the contact with the ignoble feet of a living model came as a dreadful shock to the cast-trained student.

The Italians were only a minority, though a colourful and important one. The majority of models were home grown, though one of the results of the Franco-German war according to Burne-Jones was the emigration of French models to England: 'We are inundated with Paris models, ten and twelve will call in a morning.'[18] Black models were in great demand in Paris studios according to a description of a women's atelier in the *Magazine of Art*,[19] but it was not until the beginning of the next century that England caught up with this craze. Nina Hamnett recalls drawing from a negro model at Frank Brangwyn's school before the First World War.[20] There are also occasional references to Jewish models as the century draws to its close. Given Paris's position as the art capital of the Western world at this period, it is no surprise to discover that Jewish models had entered French artistic consciousness much earlier than they did here, and that in this area as in others, the English were following a French pattern. A nasty article in *The Saturday Review* of 16 November 1895, explains how the Jewish models had overrun the Paris studios in the Second Empire until the artists had reacted against them, 'venial, scheming, grasping, ambitious, and irrepressible to a degree'. Manette Salomon, the unpleasant model heroine of the Goncourts' book of that name, was a Jew and the artist hero of Zola's *L'Oeuvre* writes the name and address of a Jewish model on his studio wall. A Jewish model turns up in *Trilby*, Mademoiselle Honorine Cahen, 'better known in the Quartier Latin as Mimi la Salope' which given the book's setting in the Paris of the 1850s is an accurate touch. This 'dirty, drabby little dolly-mop of a Jewess, a model for the figure — a very humble person indeed, socially' is taught to sing by Svengali and thus represents a sort of trial run for Trilby's experience at the hynotist's hands.[21]

The most revealing aspect of the English artists' admiration for Jewish models was that it was only Jewish women who interested them. Since there was no way that artists could make the kind of connection they did between the modern Italian male body and the sculptures and drawings done by Michelangelo, all the reasons for their taste for the Jewish female tended to be romantic in the extreme. There was a general curiosity about Jews who, fleeing continental persecution, were entering this country and its literature from the 1870s onwards. Probably the most solemn and idealizing picture of Jews in literature is George Eliot's *Daniel Deronda*, published in part form in 1876, which glamorizes the males as well as the females; but the artists' interest in the Jews was in the female of the species, and as such, closer to the novels about beautiful Jewish women with violinist fathers who led Englishmen to destruction which began to appear towards the end of the century.

The adoration of the dark woman which distinguishes so many paintings of the period also played its part, but basically what the artists saw in the Jewish models was that they wanted to see, the fulfilment of a fantasy of a woman with the female knowledge of the ages. The Goncourts had written in the 1860s that Manette Salomon had the animal sensuality that baptism seems to kill in a woman, and something of this attitude is expressed by the English painters. Wrote Burne-Jones,

Such a queer little model I had, a little Houndsditch
Jewess, self-possessed, mature and worldly and only about
twelve years old. When I said to her, 'Think of nothing and
feel silly and look wild and blow with your lips,' she threw
off Houndsditch in a moment, and thousands of years
rolled off her and she might have been born in Lebanon,
instead of the Cockney which she was.[22]

This nonsense about an adolescent who had been no further
east than Whitechapel is an insight into the almost mystical
quality this kind of model was felt to embody.

Models were not of the highest class, although the preju-
dices of the painters, the main source of information about
models, make it difficult to be sure of their precise place
in society. When a model's speech is reported it is usually
cockney. W. Graham Robertson tells a funny story about
Rossetti pointing out the beautiful mouth of the model
Fanny Cornforth, 'Miss Cornforth the while spreading her
ample charms upon a couch and throwing in an occasional
giggle, or "Oh, go along, Rissetty!".'[23] Frith reveals his
opinion of the low social status of models by remarking on
one female whose 'superiority to an ordinary model was
apparent in many ways'. It turns out to be her social superiority he is discussing: 'her manner and address were lady-
like, and her grammar never caused a shudder.'[24] Henry
Stacy Marks claimed that

occasionally gentlemen of reduced circumstances if one
might believe their own statements, were to be found in
the ranks of the models. One of them sat to me. His name
was Gordon; he had been an officer in the Light Dragoons,
and the fact of his speaking much better English than most
models gave some colour to his assertion.[25]

Much fun was had at the expense of the models' gentility.
In Grossmith's one-act play *A Commission* the humour
comes from Gloucester's mistaking the upper-class Mrs
Hemmersley for a model like himself:

Glos.   You're new to the business, ain't you.
Mrs. H. Oh, perfectly!

> *Glos.*   I thought so. Camden Town?
> *Mrs. H.* Yes.
> *Glos.*   I thought so. They all live there. Name?
> *Mrs. H.* Oh — Harris.
> *Glos.*   'Arris — Miss or Mrs?
> *Mrs. H.* Mrs.
> *Glos.*   I thought so. (Aside). They're all Mrs.[26]

Labouring and soldiering were common previous occupations for male models. Jim Bishop, a famous model of the 1850s, was discovered among a gang of labourers building houses for the artists Cope and Redgrave. According to Horsley, he was a 'powerful and well-proportioned man, with a handsome head', and he was soon posing in the Academy's life class. He was also a prize fighter,

> a line of business from which he found it necessary to retire, as not conducive to his appearance as a model, when called upon to pose for a crowned head, an inspired prophet, or a father of a family in some gentle domestic scene, such as occur in Webster's admirable works.[27]

Frith says that some of the Academy's life class models were splendid guardsmen, among them Brunskill whose magnificent physique and extraordinary endurance of painful attitudes made him a favourite until the dark day he turned up drunk.

Many of the models boosted their earnings by taking work on the side. Henry Stacy Marks wrote that 'the model will, in some cases, eke out the gains he makes by "sitting" in the day by becoming a "super" at some theatre by night'.[28] Jim Bishop kept pigs, making Landseer laugh by asking if he could get the Queen to put her leftovers aside for them.[29] Being a model included a willingness to run errands for the artists. Henry Stacy Marks describes how a sovereign could be earned by being the first model in the hall to hear the name of a newly elected academician and rushing by cab to present the artist with the good news.[30]

Models came from the poorer areas of London as befitted their working-class status. In Henry James's *The Real Thing*, the painter-narrator is approached by an ex-major and his wife, Major and Mrs Monarch, for possible modelling work: 'Their address was humble (I remember afterwards thinking it had been the only thing about them that was really professional).'[31] The Italians came from Clerkenwell because that was where the immigrants settled, the Jews from Whitechapel for the same reason. Because there were major artists' settlements in Hampstead to the north and in Chelsea, Hammersmith and Kensington to the west, the models tended to come from the nearby lower rent area. Haverstock and Lillie Roads are mentioned as a source of female models in Israel Zangwill's *The Master*, both of which had a genteel population and a closeness to the north and west side artists' colonies. For the same reason, St John's Wood and Kensington are given as areas where models live in 'Artists' Models of Modern Babylon' in *The Bohemian*.[32]

Pay was not unreasonable. A shilling an hour is a figure frequently mentioned for the mid century and one-and-nine pence is mentioned in *The Times* in 1885: a fair rate of pay for the period, a little above a housemaid's salary and way above the slavery of seamstresses, who right up to the 1890s were earning fifteen shillings for a twelve-hour day, six days a week. In a satirical piece in *Household Words* which proposed ridding the country of models, Charles Dickens computes the earnings of the broad-chested model as two shillings an hour, six hours a day, six months a year '(I take that to be high, but his chest is very large)' — and this in 1850.[33] The Christmas 1893 number of *The Bohemian* gives the average earnings of a successful model as around thirty shillings a week.

The drawback was that employment was not steady. Gilbert Burgess sums up pay and employment prospects in his contribution on artists in *Living London*, the three-volume account of London life edited by George R. Sims in 1902:

The professional model has a somewhat precarious existence. When at work, he, or she, is well paid, but it is possible for a model to be unemployed for weeks at a time; it may so happen that no painter needs his particular type.[34]

This lack of security led to the practice of collections for models down on their luck. The collections mentioned by Zangwill in fiction and Frith in fact, were examples of a wide practice, certainly on behalf of the most popular models by the more important painters. In Israèl Zangwill's *The Master*, a collection is taken for Lily:

> '*Our* Lily?' asked Greme. 'But she doesn't sit now — she's on the stage.'
> 'I know, she's dislocated her ankle, and can't dance.'
> 'She never could dance,' observed Herbert.
> 'How ever did she get an engagement?'
> 'Browney put her into his types of English beauty,' replied Cornpepper. 'But she's a good girl all the same, and she hasn't got any money. I'll lead off with five bob.'[35]

Collecting for models continues into the twentieth century. In Gilbert Cannan's *Mendel* of 1917, the novel based on the life of the painter Mark Gertler, the artists raise £50 when the model Hetty Finch gets pregnant.[36] There was a definite career structure, with models who posed at the Academy Schools or for respected artists at the top. Arthur Ransome says that models talk of artists as 'my artists' and are as happy as the painter if they can say they are in the New Gallery or the Royal Academy.[37] The Italian male models and the robust guardsmen types were the modelling stars during the Victorian period; their names crop up frequently in memoirs. Very little was said about female models, and particularly nude female models, until the loosening of manners and morals at the end of the century. The life model whose livelihood depended on a fine body would sink as the sags and bags of middle-age took over into less prestigious head, hand and character modelling.

Several English writers claimed that the most beautiful models married artist, although it is hard to think of many who did. Unlike France, where fact (Monet, Bonnard) and fiction (Zola's *L'Oeuvre*, Maupassant's *The Model*) shows marrying one's model was a frequent occurrence in artistic life, in England most of the artists were far too in awe of the conventions of the age and far too interested in advancing their careers to risk social acceptance by marrying a woman from a class beneath their own. No doubt the occasional good-looking female improved her social position through a liaison with an artist, but the majority of English artists kept one eye on their sales and the other on their status. Until the advent of Bohemian ideas at the end of the century, which made the model-artist liaison respectable, most painters in this country were too busy forging a professional identity for themselves to risk it by unconventional behaviour.

Models got work by going round the studios, as photographic models today visit the photographers and fashion editors they hope will like their looks and use them: 'Scarcely a day — certainly never a week — passes without applicants for sittings making their appearance in artists' studios, of all ages, from the baby in arms to the man of eighty', wrote Frith.[38] Communications were difficult in the days before the telephone was in general use. Appointments were made by letter if they couldn't be made in person, and cancelled by telegram. There was a grapevine of good models who were passed around the artists. The amateur artist hero of Weedon Grossmith's *A Commission* of 1904 sends the out-of-work Gloucester to sit for the costumes of a masonic group a brother artist is painting.

According to John Lavery, Scottish painters in the 1880s used to advertise for models in the *Glasgow Herald*,[39] but advertising was not a feature of London modelling life. It was only occasionally in the nineteenth century that London models advertised for work. In fact, from its foundation in 1880 until 1902, *The Artist* has only three such advertisements. The first appeared on 1 January 1888, and ran 'Female model requires more sittings. Good face, perfect figure. Address 'Clytie', 55 Beckenham Road, Penge.' Was Clytie her own name, the name of a house, or a refined way of suggesting by a reference to Watts's famous bare-breasted bust of that name that she modelled in the nude? Far from striking models round the country as a promising way to get work, no other advertisement appeared for six years, until 1 March 1894: 'Model — A respectable young person wishes for additional employment as Model to Lady Artists. Terms, one shilling per hour. Reference permitted to well-known lady artists. Address E.T., 30 Moylen Road, Hammersmith, W.' The final one appeared in February 1897: 'Artist's model — Lady, widow of professional man, would be thankful for work. Tall, good figure: unexceptionable refs. A.H. c/o The Artist.' One hopes that this model who had come down in the world fared better than Henry James's couple in *The Real Thing*, who prove less efficient at modelling the aristocrats they are than the artist's cockney model.

The benefits of advertising finally dawned on the models early in the following century. Between 1909 and 1913 *The Art Chronicle* carried at least one advertisement from a model seeking work in nearly every issue. Some of these are highly enterprising in their efforts to attract attention, although no one equalled Mr G. Wilkins who on 11 December 1909 took a quarter page advertisement of himself in eighteenth-century costume (fig. 13) with the words 'School of Art and Studio Model' under the photo. On 10 January 1913, can be found 'Model (male) art student, will pose heron still and robin bright.' On 6 December 1912, 'Model (30) artist, up against hard times, will pose; slender figure, original, interesting appearance.' On 12 January 1912, 'Young gentleman offers himself as model and domestic assistant in studio of young artist (male) in return for board and lodgings', a carbon copy of the situation in James's short story in which an Italian is model and servant. Artists also began to advertise, usually with precise specifications: 'Abundant natural red hair essential' stated an artist on 5 August 1912.

In 1912 the *Art Chronicle* set out to rectify the absence of any central structure through which artists and models could contact each other by setting up a Register of Models. Subscribers to the magazine could choose models from this book, which was kept in the *Chronicle*'s office, safe in the knowledge that any models they selected would be the bona fide variety, their credentials proved by their possession of two references from artists or art schools. Other attempts at organizing models were informal, more in the style of the woman who supplied Nollekens with country girls in the eighteenth century. Harry Furniss recalls an old woman at the end of the nineteenth century who lived by supplying artists with child models. 'One had only to write and tell the old lady what style of child was required and one was immediately presented.'[40] After the First World War, an artists' model agency was operated by Robespierre and Pichaud, 18 Addison Road, Bedford Park, offering models from 7 to 70. By 1924, their advertisements also offered artistic photographic life studies and the occasional studio for rent.

Painters saw models as actors — a fitting view in an age when reproducing scenes on canvas was what art was all about. Like actors and actresses, models were hired for their suitability for a specific part or for their versatility. In *The Real Thing*, James contrasts the professional model Miss Churm with the well-born Mrs Monarch's unsuccessful attempts at modelling:

> After I had drawn Mrs. Monarch a dozen times I perceived more clearly than before that the value of such a model as Miss Churm resided precisely in the fact that she had no positive stamp, combined of course with the other fact that what she did have was a curious and inexplicable talent for imitation. Her usual appearance was like a curtain which she could draw up at request for a capital performance . . . it was so much her pride that she could sit for characters that had nothing in common with each other.[41]

The artists' requests for specific types makes them sound like casting directors. 'Artist wants addresses of models for head types. Clean shaven detective, handsome school-boy about 14, to sit in town.' Or 'Wanted addresses, girl, pretty children, negroes, etc.'[42] Over-exposure and typecasting were real problems: Charles Dickens became very irritated at the way the same models turned up in picture after picture, describing to the Baroness Burdett-Coutts in a letter of 1845 the Roman models on the Spanish Steps who

> dispose themselves in conventionally picturesque attitudes and wait to be hired as sitters. The first time I went up there, I could not conceive how their faces were familiar to me — how they seemed to have bored me, for many years, in every variety of action and costume — and to

come back upon my sight as perfect nightmares. At last it flashed upon me all at once that we had made acquaintance, and improved it, on the walls of the Royal Academy . . . And there is not one among them whom you wouldn't know, at first sight, as well as the statue at Charing Cross.[43]

He goes on to list the assassin model 'who leans against a wall with his arms folded', the pastoral model 'who always lies asleep in the sun' and the haughty model 'who looks over his shoulder and always seems to be going away'. But his real hate was 'the most aggravating of the party', the 'dismal old patriarch, with very long white hair and beard, who carries a great staff in his hand, which staff has been faithfully copied at the Exhibition in all its twists and knots, at least once through the catalogue'. Dickens was obsessed by this particular model, referring to him again thirteen years later in an article in *Household Words* as 'the aggravating patriarch with the white beard'.[44] Dickens ends his letter with a prim avowal of his own literary practice: 'It is a good illustration of the student life as it is, that young men should go on copying these people elaborately time after time and time out of mind, and find nothing fresh or suggestive in the actual world about them.'

Once the models were chosen they had to be clothed, and a minor industry emerged in the 1870s to service this need. The Artists' Costume Supply of 40 Abingdon Road, Kensington, advertised costumes for artists models in the *Art Chronicle* of 1913, and Madame Lillian ran an advertisement in the same magazine in 1911: 'Madame Lillian — Specialist in Day, Evening, and Fancy Gowns at moderate charges. Models' costumes worked and completed to artists' designs.' Sometimes artists advertised for costumes, sometimes models offered to supply their own. An advertisement in *The Artist* of December 1897 announced that 'a fine collection of costumes, mostly historical ones, used by a well-known artist (now deceased) is to be disposed of at reasonable prices'. It is intriguing to think of Victorian painters assembling their own costume departments, but given the period's obsession with accuracy it is not surprising that artists would prefer a real Empire ball gown to an illustration in a pattern book.

In all the agonized searchings for the right face, the right body, the right accessories and the right scenery can be seen the nineteenth-century obsession with accuracy. A fictional account of this obsession appears in Anthony Trollope's *Last Chronicle of Barset* published in 1867, which contains a discussion of whether Jael should wear jewellery in the painting *Jael and Sisera*. The painter thought not

> But when Mrs. Broughton discovered from her Bible that Heber had been connected by family ties with Moses, she was more than ever sure that Heber's wife would have in her tent much of the spoilings of the Egyptians. And when Clara van Siever suggested that at any rate she would not have worn them in a time of confusion when soldiers were loose, flying about the country, Mrs. Broughton was quite confident that she would have put them on before she invited the captain of the enemy's host into her tent.[45]

The passage is comic but the evidence of the artists' memoirs, not to mention the paintings themselves, shows it was a parody of a common discussion in English studios of the period. A link was made between the quality of the picture and the quality of the model it was copied from — a link which might seem less naive in the light of the strivings after period accuracy and facial credibility in serials produced by television drama departments today.

In the 1890s the modelling and theatrical worlds briefly touched on each other. The cause was the music-hall entertainment known as Living Pictures, famous paintings posed by actors and actresses in the manner still practised by the *Folies Bergère* today. Many of the paintings chosen for the stage were well-known and worthy, like Sir Luke Fildes's *The Doctor*, a picture which had received a great deal of admiration at the 1891 Academy for its pathetic scene of a doctor watching a child through the crisis of its illness. But the living pictures really took off with the Kilyani Troupe's *tableaux vivants* at London's Palace Theatre, which were not so high-minded. A report in *The Stage* of 26 October 1893 gives the flavour of the type of pictures in which this troupe specialized:

The first shown is 'Diana', represented by Mdlle. Ella, a beautiful picture. Next is 'Moonlight' a very effective grouping by Mdlle. Annita and Rodolphe. Mdlle. Lily makes a bold picture as Sappho, standing in defiant attitude on the staircase. Sweetly pretty is 'The Fairy of the Moon', represented by Mdlle. Alma, and 'Milo's Venus' (Mdlle. Ella) rouses the audience to loud applause ... The Venus de Medicis of Mddle. Ella brings forth a series of 'Oh's' from the audience. Mdlles. Annita and Alma show in 'The Daughter of the Sheikh,' and 'Faith, Hope and Charity' is the theme set forth by Mdlles. Audrie, Lily and Saida. An extremely effective picture is 'Psyche and Cupid', by Mdlle. Annita and Rodolphe and Mdlle. Ella's 'Ariane' is very good indeed. 'Una and the Lion' is the seventeenth picture, and the last and crowning representation is 'Aphrodite' by Mdlle. Alma. The sight of this caused much enthusiasm amongst those in front.

These living pictures caused trouble as well as enthusiasm. Owners of the copyright of the paintings brought suits against the theatres which, they felt, were making money from pictures they did not own, and against the newspapers which ran drawings of the *tableaux* in their pages. The purity campaigners were vocal in their disapproval of the indecency theatre managements were allowing on to their boards. The complaints led George Bernard Shaw to pay five shillings at the Palace Theatre box office to go and see for himself; he produced out of the experience a devastating attack in *The Saturday Review* on the purity campaigners which concluded

for I notice that the semi-nudity which is quite a common spectacle in the case of male athletes is not complained of, though, if there were anything in the Vigilance Association's view of such exhibitions as demoralizing, our women ought by this time to be more demoralized than our men.

He also pointed out that 'It was only too obvious to a practised art critic's eye that what was presented as flesh was really spun silk.'[46]

The job of posing in flesh-coloured silk on a music-hall

stage was not unrelated to posing in the nude in a studio, and the advertisement columns of the art and theatre magazines show a little flurry of awareness of this fact. In the 2 April 1894 issue of *The Artist* the following notice appeared: 'WANTED — Artists' models for tableaux vivants to tour in provinces. Engagement six weeks certain but might last several months. Railway fares paid: send photo with application.' It is hard to know why an art magazine was chosen for this advertisement. Possibly it was thought that models would be more skilled at holding poses than their actress or ballet girl counterparts. Perhaps, such posing was felt to be below the dignity of actors and actresses. Or perhaps the models required were the life-class variety, for those *tableaux* beyond even a chorus girl's limits where a young lady, impersonating for example, Henrietta Rae's *Naiad*, would have no more than a flesh-coloured form-fitting garment between her naked body and the audience's eyes. Perhaps it was felt that models would accept a lower salary than actors. *The Era's* advertisements are blunt on the mean payment they offered the most multi-talented music-hall artists: 'Wanted for burlesque tour, funny comedian and several dancing young ladies for important parts. Must sing, dance and dress parts well . . . No fares advanced. Fullest particulars, photos and terms (must be very low) for long tour.'

For a little while after this, artists' models tried advertising in the theatrical papers. On 5 and 18 May 1894, the miscelleneous column of *The Era* carried the advertisement 'Wanted, employment as artists' model by lady, highest ref.', but just why a lady imagined that artists would read the jobs wanted column of a theatrical magazine, in which bill posters, wardrobe mistresses and managers with new plays offered their wares, is difficult to see. Presumably the living pictures craze had given her the idea; more practical thinking was evidenced by the model who advertised in *The Era* of 26 May 1895: 'Wanted, engagement for tableau vivant by artist's model (male), London or tour, height 6'. Fine figure, good poser.' However, when four weeks later someone for a *tableau vivant* was required in *The Era* a model was not specified though sobriety was: 'Wanted, gentleman, about 5' 10" for characters in living pictures. Sobriety and respectability indispensable.'

Artists' models did not extend their employment opportunities through living pictures. The stage was an overcrowded profession and the jobs vacant columns of *The Era* show that it was hard enough for actors and actresses to get work without allowing others into their profession. It was far more likely that a music-hall performer with a pretty face, good figure and a passable talent for singing and dancing would take part in a *tableau vivant* as an extension of her theatrical activities than that an artist's model would take part in one as an extension of hers. The interviewer of music-hall artiste Minnie Rose in *The Bohemian* of 1895 suggested that her grace and charms made her a candidate for *tableaux vivants*.[47]

Significantly, no one on *The Bohemian*'s staff considered interviewing artists' models; they were clearly lower down the social scale than chorus girls. Harry Furniss reveals that becoming a chorus girl was a step up out of modelling:

> The marriage of chorus girls, girls who came out of shops and restaurants, or pastry-cooks perhaps out of the kitchen, or from art studios, where they sat for the 'altogether', and from thence on to the stage, and wear beautiful gowns or beautiful tights as the case may be, bring fresh life, no doubt, into the used-up noble scions of our ancient nobility.[48]

After almost ten years' modelling, Furniss's model took singing and dancing lessons as preparation for going on the stage. Instead of achieving stardom she married a successful low comedian who beat her up.

Music-hall performers and artists used each other at this period. The beautiful actress Ellen Terry who in 1864 was married for a year to the painter G.F. Watts had set the trend by having her portrait painted many times by many artists. Years later, and lower down the social scale, *The Bohemian* reported that Minnie Rose had sat for the head of Galatea in a picture of Pygmalion and Galatea. Actresses saw modelling as a way of forwarding their careers. Prints of paintings for which they had posed put them in the public eye as did having their photographs reproduced as postcards. It says volumes for the difference in status between models and actresses that in the encyclopaedic picture-postcard series that mushroomed round the turn of the century there were several devoted to music-hall actresses but not one to artists' models.

Artists benefited financially from the connection by having their paintings of pretty actresses reproduced as prints. It was a nineteenth-century artist's dream to launch a new type of female beauty and they were ever on the look-out for the girl who would help them make this dream come true. Artists lived in hope of emulating Rossetti, Whistler or Burne-Jones and having a brand of female beauty named after them. Clinch in Zangwill's *The Master* dreams of launching 'une femme de Clinch' on the world.[49]

Away from the ranks of professional models, the artists had to put themselves in the hands of amateurs. John Callcott Horsley, the Royal Academician whose recollections were published in 1903, writes that at his house in Kent,

> when removed from the region of professional models, I was most fortunate in finding several charming young people, who sat to me again and again, showing the most admirable patience, and also a kindly and intelligent interest in their arduous task.[50]

The lack of professional models was a constant headache for the artist and theatrical designer W. Graham Robertson who shared a house at Sandhills for a few years at the end of the 1880s with the Scottish painter Arthur Melville. Robertson posed as Christ for Melville, hanging by his hands from two ropes high up in the studio gallery, a job which he was very happy to turn over to a 'charming Italian organ grinder whom a kindly fate sent our way' (from the Italian colony at Godalming) 'and who become model-in-chief to both Arthur and myself for two years, his mother going round with the organ in his absence'.[51] The fact that after Antonio returned to Italy with his savings he was replaced by a beautiful London model called Bessie who came to stay for weeks at a time, shows how dependent the artists were on good models. When Sir Hubert Herkomer opened his art school in the 1890s in Bushey in Hertfordshire, miles away from professional models, local villagers would cluster outside the gate each morning in the hope of being hired to pose. Children were paid half rate while tramps would sit for practically nothing.[52]

But even artists with access to professional models would take up an amateur model because the face fit the conception of what was wanted on canvas. Frith was always on the lookout for suitable non-professionals, and the assorted London types he imported into his studio, from elderly Jews through boy crossing-sweepers to lady orange-sellers were a rich source of anecdote. Frith was one of those artists who tended to go for the real thing (doubtless it was to show his distance from such a conception of realism that James gave his story that title), hiring real acrobats, for example, to model for the acrobats in the foreground of his famous *Derby Day* painting. The amateurs seem to have caused much more trouble than the professionals and the stories about them — the acrobat felt faint as he posed, the crossing-sweeper stole — throw a flattering light on the behaviour of the professionals.

Artists felt free to take their models from anywhere. A joke in *Punch* for 30 July 1887 shows two outraged artists reading a proclamation from the school authorities forbidding them to take children out of school since their education was suffering. My grandfather is the living proof that artists plucked children from schools. He recalls being picked to model by an important artist who came to the Jewish Free School in the Whitechapel of the mid 1890s and went through all the classes looking for a suitably semitic child to model nude for a biblical painting. Having explained to my grandfather what he wanted, he drove to the family house in Fournier Street, which though grand for Whitechapel was not so grand that its status couldn't be upped immeasurably by a carriage and pair outside. Once a week for six weeks after this my grandfather was collected from home and taken by carriage to a house in St John's Wood which to his nine-year-old eyes was palatial with statues, paintings and velvet curtains. In the studio he modelled in the nude for half an hour with the painter barking 'you moved' every few minutes. Once, he recalls, a lady model appeared only to be told by the painter to go away as she was ten minutes early. The sitting over, he was taken by the housekeeper to the kitchen where he was given a lavish tea, then home by carriage to Whitechapel. Payment took the form of a weekly postal order sent to Fournier Street, but how much it was for he was never told.

One of the interesting things about this story is the lengths to which the painter had to go, as a gentleman of position, to treat his non-professional model well. Permission from the parents, the presence of the housekeeper, the highly visible carriage and pair were all ways to remove any hint of scandal from the potentially explosive situation of a respected male painter alone with a naked nine-year-old boy.

Female non-professionals gave rise to a different set of problems. Although what might be called the democracy of beauty meant that, in theory, pretty women of all classes were there for the artists' choosing, contacting ladies of promising appearance was not easy for artists. The tone of the accounts of getting women to sit tends to split along class lines: for every comic account of inviting a lower-class woman to pose there is a parallel version in tones of high seriousness of arranging for a lady to sit. Georgiana Burne-Jones recalls her husband spying a girl he wished to paint at a Wagner rehearsal at the Albert Hall:

> When the rehearsal was over he turned to Mr. Richard Grosvenor who happened to be sitting near us, and said 'If only I could make some studies from her.' 'I'll ask if you may,' was the answer, and to our amazement he went directly to the young lady and her mother, who were just going out. We saw him join them and disappear but knew no more till the next day. Then Mr. Grosvenor came to tell us that, curiously enough, he had been able to do some little service for the ladies as they were entering the hall the day before, and so had earned a right to claim their attention afterwards, and that in the kindest possible way Edward's request had been granted. 'She has often been called my "Burne-Jones' daughter",' said the mother with quiet understanding of the incident.[53]

For many aspiring or actual academicians of the nineteenth century, approaching a likely model was akin to picking up a woman and therefore something that might reflect badly on their professional status. Describing the difficulty of finding the right models 'to enable one's ideal to be realised', Horsley made a plea for the artist to be able to approach any owner of the 'faultless form or fascinating feature' which might help this ideal on to canvas: 'My contention is that no properly constituted male or female ought to be offended by being asked to sit as a model.'[54] Payment was a problem. The artist could hardly offer the non-professional upper-class sitter a shilling an hour plus studio lunch. For such women a drawing, a print or the friendship of the artist were suitable rewards.

Horsley was not the only artist who felt his status as an artist depended on impeccable social behaviour, but it was not till the change in thinking which accompanied the acceptance of Bohemian ideas at the end of the century, that the propriety of approaching a promising female model became a less knotty problem of artistic conduct. Doubtless it was as difficult as ever for the shy artist to approach a pretty woman, but after the advent of Bohemian ideas the cause would be diffidence and not fear of weakening his status or offending the person approached.

In this connection the behaviour of the Pre-Raphaelites, the one truly Bohemian group of nineteenth-century English artists, is revealing. In *My Grandfather, His Wives and Loves* Diana Holman Hunt has described how the Pre-Raphaelites engaged in the sport of model hunting: 'They roamed the streets with arms linked pursuing their prey ... Pretty girls were surrounded and captured like birds in a net.'[55] But it is only in this century that such accounts of the painters' unconventional behaviour have become acceptable. At the time, whatever the state of their private lives, the Pre-Raphaelites kept a nervous eye on their public, as was shown by Holman Hunt's terror in 1858 lest 'Calmuck', a comic tale about an artist, a model and a jealous husband by Robert Brough in *Household Words* with the conclusion 'This is a true story', be pinned on him.[56] Diana Holman Hunt says that 'Calmuck' was a satirical account of Holman Hunt's affair with Emma Watkins, the field girl he had painted in *The Hireling Shepherd*, and that he went so far in the interests of keeping his reputation clean as to ask Charles Dickens, who was the editor, to print an apology. Dickens refused on the grounds that this would arouse even more interest.[57] Despite the immense importance of the good female model to the painter, her presence and his dependence were an embarrassment to the artist in a period which had no way to account for the intimacy between a low-class woman and an educated man except in the basest terms.

There is no doubt that models were necessary to painters in the second half of the nineteenth century. Frith's frustrated moans when they arrived late for a sitting, or drunk, or when he could not find a suitable one for the picture he had in hand, make that crystal clear:

> My diary for 1850 presents the usual record of foggy days and disappointing models; in short, difficulties without number more or less successfully battled with. As I could not have Hogarth to sit for me [he was about to paint Hogarth before the Governor of Calais] I had to keep a bright look-out for someone resembling him.[58]

A tone of strained good humour marks the tales of the models told by the artists. It is remarkable how many of their stories centre on their cheekiness or drunkeness and how few tell of anything factual such as where they lived or what they earned. The partial nature of the artists' 'facts' about their models reveals a great deal about the artist-model relationship. Frith tells the tale of Bredman who extorted clothes and money for his non-existent wife from artists:

> The man's character became too well known in the profession for the calling of model to be any longer possible to him, and, strange as it may appear, though his career as a hypocritical knave was well known to us, a sufficient sum was subscribed by artists to enable him to go to Australia. He found his way to the diggings which were in full swing at that time; and I received a grateful letter from him, still in my possession, in which he informed me he was prospering . . . helping the good cause by the sale of religious goods in a store at Ballarat.[59]

This story with its boast of a well-earned testimonial — 'received a grateful letter from him — still in my possession' — is the key to much of the writing about models by the artists who used them at this period. It shows how the artists felt themselves to be superior to the models, a set of people who were in a different class from themselves, and yet with whom they were forced to be on terms of intimacy and dependence. As Burne-Jones said, 'there is no class so undesirable to be in the hands of'.[60] Resenting their dependence on such lower-class inadequates, it is no wonder that the artists' facts about models took the form they did. Necessary, but a source of problems, they were the subject of dinner-party stories told in tones of amused and exasperated paternalism. 'A chapter may well be devoted to the humours and eccentricities of models' wrote Henry Stacy Marks.[61]

Their refusal to know their place caused much irritation. The trouble was that while their class put them on a par with the servants, the service they offered and their independence made it impossible for them to be treated as servants. The difference between servants and models is neatly expressed by Frith: 'I have been able to secure the services of some of my servants as models — a practice I don't recommend, because it is apt to "turn their heads" a little, and to make them careless over less agreeable duties.'[62] Many painters were not sure the models should be in their homes at all. Horsley says that the famous Jim Bishop was strictly honest, 'at least I have never heard a word to the contrary from any of many friends in whose houses and gardens he was a familiar figure'.[63] In fact painters probably ran more risk of theft with the picturesque non-professionals hauled in off the street. Frith's boy crossing-sweeper attempted to rob him.

One way the artists' uneasiness about models was expressed was by undercutting the models' claims to professionalism. On the surface the painters recognized and referred to this professionalism. But if it meant admitting the models to some sort of equality then the artists turned the professionalism into joke. A sort of guerrilla war against the models' professional pretensions is constantly waged. Much of the humour in Grossmith's *A Commission* stems from the model's constant references to the painters as Johnnie Millais and Teddy Poynter while calling himself Mr Gloucester.

In his autobiography, Grossmith says he based Gloucester on a popular model called Foster who while sitting would begin a conversation with a reference to the President of the Royal Academy: 'Teddy Leighton . . . was rather humorous the other day, quite the exception for him.'[64] Stacy Marks wrote that

> I have had many models in my time, chiefly of the male genus. They are generally vain, and are firmly convinced that the artist owes much of the success of his pictures to the fact of their having sat to him, and assert at least their equality to him by speaking of him by his surname only.[65]

Artists at this period were moving up in the world. On 21 July 1880, *Punch* published a cartoon called 'Studies in Evolution: The Artist' which shows the old-style artist in the Pig and Whistle and the new-style artist at Her Grace's Garden Party. Always a barometer of social change, *Punch* in a joke of 25 March 1882, summed up the way artists were consolidating their professional status: '*Self Satisfied Amateur (showing his drawing to our Artist, R.A.)* "And recollect I'm not in the TRADE, mind yer. I'm a hosier by Profession!" '

Association with models posed a problem to aspiring members of the artistic establishment, akin to the embarrassment of millionaires whose fortunes had been founded on such unglamorous objects as patent medicines or brass bedsteads. Like the new millionaires trying to put a space between the source of their fortune and themselves, the artists were dedicated to keeping a distance between themselves and their models. A joke in *Punch* of 12 December 1874 ironically entitled 'Brothers in Art' makes this division clear (fig. 11):

> *Playful R.A. (to his Model, who has been expatiating on the dignity of the Working Man)* I am pleased to perceive, Jakes, that you are content with your humble condition, and do not envy the lot of the superior classes!
> *Jakes* Henvy 'em! Why, bless yer, them as belongs to them classes as you alludes to ain't 'alf so much to be

henvied as them that belongs to the class as *Me* and YOU belongs to.

The line of demarcation expressed metaphorically in the jokes and anecdotes was built in a material sense into the grandest artists' houses at the period. An advertisement in *The Artist* of May 1884 offers a semi-detached house for rent with studio and separate models' entrance. This sensitivity to the social nuances of the artists' life by the substitution of models for servants may have been no more than a house agent's brainwave. But in fact from 1875 in Melbury Road, Fitzjohn's Avenue and Frognal, the architect Richard Norman Shaw had been building London houses for artists with a separate models' entrance which led straight from the street to the studio, thereby sparing the artist's family the strain of meeting a model on the stairs. The artist could get away with such meetings in the course of professional duties, but there was no need to inflict these low-class but socially buoyant people on the gracious life he had given his family.

Notes

1 Quentin Crisp, *The Naked Civil Servant*, (Fontana, 1977), p. 129.
2 Arthur Ransome, *Bohemia in London* (London, 1907), p. 67.
3 Estella Canziani, *Round About Three Palace Green* (London, 1939), p. 157.
4 John Callcott Horsley, RA, *Recollections of a Royal Academician* (London, 1903), p. 299.
5 W.P. Frith, *My Autobiography and Reminiscences* (3 vols., London, 1887), vol. 1, p. 57.
6 Elizabeth Butler, *An Autobiography* (London, 1922), p. 44.
7 W.G. Robertson, *Time Was* (London, 1931), p. 236.
8 Canziani, *Round About*, p. 157.
9 Harry Furniss, *Some Victorian Women* (London, 1923), p. 104.
10 Georgiana Burne-Jones, *Memorials of Edward Burne-Jones* (2 vols., London, 1904), vol. 1, page 262.
11 Robertson, *Time Was*, p. 39.
12 Frank Hyde, 'Anticoli Corrado, A Town of Models', *The International Studio*, September, 1912.
13 Dubosc, modèle, *Soixante ans dans les ateliers des artistes* (Paris, 1900), ch. 8.
14 Frith, *My Autobiography*, vol. 2, p. 50.
15 Burne-Jones, *Memorials*, vol. 1, p. 262.

16 Dr Angelo S. Rappoport, *Famous Artists and Their Models* (London, 1913), p. 6.
17 Edward J. Poynter, RA., *Ten Lectures on Art* (London, 1879), Lecture 3, p. 42.
18 Burne-Jones, *Memorials*, vol. 2, p. 16.
19 Barclay Day, 'Studio Life in Paris', *Magazine of Art* (London), vol. 5, 1862, p. 511.
20 Nina Hamnett, *Laughing Torso* (London, 1932), p. 20.
21 George Du Maurier, *Trilby*, 1894 (Dent, 1956), part 2, p. 46.
22 Burne-Jones, *Memorials*, vol. 2, p. 215.
23 Robertson, *Time Was*, p. 291.
24 Frith, *My Autobiography*, vol. 2, p. 3.
25 Henry Stacy Marks, *Pen and Pencil Sketches* (2 vols., London, 1894), vol. 2, pp. 116-17.
26 Weedon Grossmith, *A Commission* (London, 1904), p. 16. First performed 6 June 1891.
27 Horsley, *Recollections*, pp. 298-9.
28 Marks, *Pen and Pencil*, vol. 2, p. 115.
29 Frith, *My Autobiography*, vol. 1, p. 278.
30 Marks, *Pen and Pencil*, vol. 1, p. 230.
31 Henry James, *The Real Thing*, 1892 (Macmillan, 1893), p. 19.
32 Amateur, 'Artists' Models of Modern Babylon', *The Bohemian*, Christmas no. 1893, pp. 62-3.
33 Charles Dickens, 'An Idea of Mine', *Household Words*, 13 March 1858, p. 290.
34 George R. Sims, ed., *Living London* (3 vols., London, 1904-6), vol. 1, p. 124.
35 Israel Zangwill, *The Master* (London, 1895), p. 190.
36 Dennis Cannan, *Mendel* (London, 1916), Book 2, ch. 1.
37 Ransome, *Bohemia*, p. 73.
38 Frith, *My Autobiography*, vol. 2, p. 215.
39 John Lavery, *The Life of a Painter* (London, 1940), p. 43.
40 Furniss, *Some Victorian Women*, p. 106.
41 James, *The Real Thing*, pp. 22-3.
42 *The Art Chronicle*, 20 August and 10 September 1910.
43 E. Johnson, ed., *Letters from Charles Dickens to Angela Burdett-Coutts* (Jonathan Cape, 1953), p. 66.
44 Dickens, 'An Idea of Mine', p. 289.
45 Anthony Trollope, *Last Chronicle of Barset* (London, 1867) 'Jael'.
46 George Bernard Shaw, 'The Living Pictures', *The Saturday Review*, 6 April 1895.
47 'A Priestess Pro Tem', *The Bohemian*, August 1895.
48 Furniss, *Some Victorian Women*, p. 58.
49 Zangwill, *The Master*, p. 171.
50 Horsley, *Recollections*, p. 343.
51 Robertson, *Time Was*, p. 302.
52 R. Morton Nance, 'Bushey Models', *The Studio*, Winter no. 1896-7, pp. 37-8.

53 Burne-Jones, *Memorials*, vol. 2, pp. 80-1.
54 Horsley, *Recollections*, p. 344.
55 Diana Holman Hunt, *My Grandfather, His Wives and Loves* (Hamish Hamilton, 1969), p. 62.
56 'Calmuck', *Household Words*, 3 April 1858, p. 365.
57 Holman Hunt, *My Grandfather*, pp. 190-4.
58 Frith, *My Autobiography*, vol. 1, p. 206.
59 Ibid., vol. 2, p. 63.
60 Burne-Jones, *Memorials*, vol. 2, p. 188.
61 Marks, *Pen and Pencil*, vol. 2, p. 114.
62 Frith, *My Autobiography*, vol. 2, p. 248.
63 Horsley, *Recollections*, p. 298.
64 Weedon Grossmith, *From Studio to Stage* (London, 1913) p. 39.
65 Marks, *Pen and Pencil*, vol. 2, pp. 114-15.

4
The Model's Status

Victorian artists' attempts to put a gap between themselves and their models shows that models have not always enjoyed the status outsiders so generously ascribe to them. Even before the second half of the nineteenth century, artists' admiring references to well-made models have something of a double-edged air about them. Leslie's 'remarkably fine' cripple suggests that the model's prize-animal qualities were uppermost in the artist's mind. And Constable's letter to Leslie of 25 February 1837, discussing plans for his month as the Visitor in the Academy's life class shows how the link of nude models with prostitution diminished their chance of being treated with dignity.

> The next week I have a little girl aged 17. She is *procured* by Etty our grand 'curator' — and I am to have her maiden 'sitting' on Monday week — his note is amusing in which he announces his decision —
> DEAR CONSTABLE
> A young figure is brought to me — who is very desirous of becoming a model — She is very like the Antigone and *all in front memorably fine*.[1]

From the start models have had a rocky status in this country. They came into its eighteenth-century schools and studios trailing clouds of the ambivalent attitudes which had surrounded them in countries whose art had reached its peak and whose academies had their teaching formulas well organized. This ambivalence stemmed from confusions about the importance of the model's role. It was first expressed by the Renaissance theorists through their belief that the finest art was based on a mastery of a number of skills — perspective, composition, imagination, anatomical knowledge, familiarity with the works of the great artists — of which drawing from life was only one.

Vasari's writings which with Michelangelo's personality and Leonardo's theory, as Pevsner has explained in *Academies of Art*, influenced the teaching programmes of the sixteenth-century Italian academies, and through them the European academies that followed, are imbued with the belief that copying from life is not enough in learning to create a work of art.[2]

Vasari believed in an art which is lifelike but without life's flaws. Although he praised Titian's painting of a nude Saint Sebastian as

> portrayed from life whose fine limbs and trunk are conveyed without artifice, all being presented just as Titian saw it in nature, so that the body of Saint Sebastian seems as if printed from a living figure it is so flesh-like and natural[3]

this unadulterated admiration of likeness to life has to be taken as a compliment to Titian's skill and not as advocacy of painting from the model.

Vasari reserved his highest praise for art that was illusionistic but which transcended the reality of the model on which it was based. At one point he actually conceived of drawing from the model as hampering to an artist:

> The painter becomes a slave if he has to keep a nude or draped model in front of him all the time he is working . . . Moreover, the use of drawings furnishes the artist's mind with beautiful conceptions and helps him to depict everything in the natural world from memory; he has no need to keep his subject in front of him all the time or to conceal under the charm of his colouring his lack of knowledge of how to draw, as for many years (having never seen Rome or any completely perfect works of art) did the Venetian painters Giorgione, Palma, Pordenone and the rest.[4]

For all his belief in working from the nude model as an

aid in learning to draw, Vasari nowhere states that successful art can be based only on that. To read Vasari is to understand how drawing from life had to fight to hold its place with the study of the antique, the knowledge of anatomy and the practice of generalizing and perfecting. Drawing from life, which included copying the flaws of ordinary human beings, benefited from a study of great ancient and modern works of art, which excluded them:

> for if an artist has not drawn a great deal and studied carefully selected ancient and modern works he cannot by himself work well from memory or enhance what he copies from life, and so give his work the grace and perfection of art which are beyond the reach of nature, some of whose aspects tend to be less than beautiful.[5]

Raphael is held up as an example of an artist who studied anatomy in order to improve the nude drawings he had formerly copied from models:

> At the time when Raphael determined to change and improve his style he had never studied the nude as intensely as it requires, for he had only copied it from life, employing the methods he had seen used by Perugino, although he gave his figures a grace that he understood instinctively. So he began to study the nude form and to compare the muscles as revealed in anatomical drawings or dissected corpses with them as they are seen, less starkly defined, in the living body. He also studied the articulation of the bones, nerves and veins, and he mastered all the points that a great painter needs to know.[6]

Michelangelo is admired for practising the principle of selection, a practice which involved drawing from several models in order to evolve an idea of the perfect form: 'only by copying the human form, and by selecting from what was beautiful the most beautiful, could he achieve perfection'.[7]

Vasari's theoretical beliefs, with their cautious endorsement of the model's role, entered England through the Royal Academy Schools. Though meticulous copying from casts and then life was seen as the basis of the students' skill, when it came to the final painting or sculpture, nature was not to be copied but improved with the aid of imagination.

This belief that the final work of art had to shake free of its origins explains the surprisingly dismissive way the eighteenth-century artists speak about the model to their students. In a speech in which he claims the superiority of knowledge of anatomy and proportion over the mere sense of sight, the Academician John Opie was forging the English link in the chain of art theory which began with the Italian Renaissance:

> for if, in such cases, the eye alone be insufficient to enable him to render them correctly, how much more so must it prove, in regard to figures enlivened by sentiment, or agitated by contending passions, and thrown into sudden, animated and momentary action, in which a living model (if capable of being placed at all) can hold but for an instant, and must quickly sink into quiescent torpidity! ... If not familiar with the rules of proportion, ponderation, and the just division and balance of motion in every joint and limb, he will find it impossible to 'catch the Cynthia of the minute'; his labour will be in vain; his living model, far from proving a useful pattern, will rather tend to lead him astray, and his (under such circumstances) presumptuous attempt at drawing must inevitably be deficient in precision, correctness, energy and grace.[8]

In no department was the model's role more likely to be undercut than in the Plaster Academy, whose casts provided the eighteenth century's greatest rivals to the life class models. Because progression from casts to life was not automatic but depended on satisfying the instructors, many students took a long time to reach the life school. Furthermore, when they arrived there they could only stay by keeping their standards up. So that while drawing from life was the apex of achievement, the reality for many students was drawing from casts of others' work.

An admiration of earlier works of art was a major plank in the eighteenth-century aesthetic. Connoisseurs as well as students carried a mental picture of the classical sculptures to use as a measurement for judging other works of art.

It is impossible to overestimate the importance held by casts at this stage in the nation's artistic consciousness. Evidence comes from Joseph Wright of Derby whose two paintings of artistic subjects both show casts of classical sculptures. In *An Academy by Lamplight c.* 1768-9 (Mr and Mrs Paul Mellon) a group of boys draws the Nymph with a Shell with the Borghese Gladiator in the background, and in *Three Persons Viewing the Gladiator by Lamplight c.* 1764-5 (private collection, UK), the men study a small-scale representation of the Borghese Gladiator. Haskell and Penny in *Taste and the Antique* say that 'the Gladiator was particularly admired for the truthful rendering of anatomy'.[9]

As Haskell and Penny have shown, commercial production of casts was getting into its stride at this period. Knowledge of casts was proof of membership of an eighteenth-century cultural club, the fine art equivalent of having read the classical authors in the original. Possession of casts was even better, and some great collections of antiquities and reproductions were formed in the second half of the eighteenth century. The connoisseurs of the period worshipped their statues for their perfection and occasionally went so far as to wish life on them, as can be seen in Wright's *An Academy by Lamplight*. At first glance the Nymph looks as though she is real, an illusion which was not a product of Wright's fantasy but an effect aimed at by the owners of such statuary. An account of the Townley Collection of Greek and Roman art formed in the 1770s in the *General Chronicle and Literary Magazine* of May 1812 says that 'lamps were placed to form the happiest contrast of light and shade; and the improved effect of the marbles amounted, by these means, almost to animation . . .'[10]

Something of the universal truths casts were felt to embody can be gathered from a presidental discourse Benjamin West gave to the Academy students in 1794:

Were the young artist, in like manner, to propose to himself a subject in which he would represent the peculiar excellencies of women, would he not say, that these excellencies consist in a virtuous mind, a modest mien, a tranquil deportment, and a gracefulness in motion? And in embodying the combined beauty of these qualities, would he not bestow on the figure a general, smooth, and round fulness of form, to indicate the softness of character; bend the head gently forward, in the common attitude of modesty; and awaken our ideas of the slow and graceful movements peculiar to the sex, by limbs free from that masculine and sinewy expression which is the consequence of active exercise? — and such is the Venus de Medici.[11]

No self-respecting Academy of Arts could be without its collection of casts and the Royal Academy was no exception. A guide to the casts of the Royal Academy was published in 1783 in which the author Joseph Baretti, the Academy's Secretary for foreign correspondence, suggests the inspirational role they could play in the creation of the English school of painting:

> Such are the embellishments of the new Seminary of the Arts and such the Models it contains for its improvement, the Originals of which have long been the delight and wonder of Mankind. Let us confidently hope in the present hour of Royal Patronage, that productions of equal perfection will soon be added to them by the rising genius of the English School.[12]

Notice that models here means casts.

Far from being no more than a middle stage in the art student's education, drawing from casts was seen as enormously important in forming the student's ability to produce the correct kind of finished work. Even though drawing from life was the goal, the aesthetic ensured that the classical statues seemed far greater than the nude models who aped them in the poses they adopted. Because the casts supplied a frame into which the faulty human body could be fitted, knowledge of the great sculptures would prevent the student from being seduced into copying the imperfections of the live model.

The practice of reconciling the real and ideal continued into Victorian art schools; but by then it had turned from an article of artistic faith into a problem.

In 1863, William Mulready was asked by a Royal Commission on the position of the Royal Academy in relation to the fine arts, whether students painted the deficiencies of the living model or idealized and refined it. His reply gives a fascinating insight into the mental juggling involved in reconciling the contemporary aesthetic of meticulous copying with the previous century's idealizing aesthetic:

> I suggest to them the absolute necessity of beginning by following the model closely and getting its characteristics truly drawn in outline; then, if I think there is anything very imperfect in the model's form, I say that I think it is very imperfect, and I even try to show the students how that imperfection arose in the figure, whether it was the original formation of the infant, or whether it resulted from the practice of the model's profession; and I also endeavour to show the students how far such a deviation from perfection being characteristic, it would in certain classes of art be a proper feature to make a point of ... I should also tell the students, if they had but lately come from the antique to the life school, not to be governed entirely by their recollection of the antique and its purity of form when they had the model before them, but to think of the model's differences from that class of antique to which it naturally belonged. I might, if the student were very intelligent, say to what extent he might venture in a figure which was Apollo-like, to lean perhaps a little more than the model did towards the Apollo Belvedere, and so on;[13]

Even the Slade, founded with the aim of presenting a more modern curriculum than the Academy, could not completely let go of the notion of the ideal when it came to life drawing. The Slade's innovation was to make life drawing accessible to its students much sooner than the Academy Schools did — sometimes after only weeks instead of years — in an effort to get away from what was seen as the pernicious effects of constantly drawing from casts. But in the address with which he opened the Slade, Poynter shows he was still haunted by the problem of reconciling the real and ideal which the nude model in the life class posed:

> although you will find nothing in the antique which you

cannot find in nature, there is much, even in the best models, which you will not see in the antique, and it is precisely these points which make the difficulty in drawing from nature, and which render it necessary for the student to have some acquaintance with the general character and proportions of the human figure before attempting the study of the living model.[14]

While the casts helped keep models in their place in the eighteenth century, the artists' patronizing attitude towards their models' stupidity, amusing antics and social aspirations achieved this aim in the nineteenth. On top of this, female models had an extra slur on their status with which to contend, one which was all their own: their alleged connection with sexual immorality.

Unlike the clash with the casts in the eighteenth century or the class consciousness of the nineteenth century, the link with immorality is as old as written art history. An aura of sexuality has always surrounded the female model. The fact that until this century the women who earned their living from modelling were drawn from the lower classes boosted the notion of their sexual availability, as did the fact that theirs was a job no respectable woman could undertake.

The link between models and immorality frequently becomes a link between modelling and prostitution; a connection established in the anecdotes of prostitutes modelling for artists by classical Greek writers. Its strength in eighteenth-century England is shown by the briefest assembly of assorted remarks and drawings. Smith said that Nollekens's nude 'Venuses' were supplied by the local madam. In his *Treatise on Painting*, Hogarth described Cheron and Vanderbank's Academy in the 1720s as having 'a woman figure to make it more inviting to subscribers'.[15] Edward Edwards in *Anecdotes of Painters* (1808), says that the early eighteenth-century public considered life schools to be 'held for immoral purposes'.[16] Thomas Rowlandson slashed at Lady Emma Hamilton's reputation by showing her modelling nude as a young girl before a group of men who are more interested in ogling her than drawing her (fig. 6). In the nineteenth century the link was kept alive by the comparison the purity campaigners made between modelling and prostitution. And it survives today in the 'model' signs prostitutes put next to their doorbells.

Victoria's reign saw the peak of unease surrounding the question of the female nude model. Just as Victorians divided women into the good and the bad, those who did and those who did not, so those connected with the arts divided models into those who modelled in the nude and those who did not. Wrote Weedon Grossmith, ex-artist, actor/playwright and urbanity itself in *From Studio to Stage*:

> In my experience, the generality of models are hard working respectable girls. But there are two distinct classes of models, those who sit for the figure and those who are draped and who only sit for costume or for the face and hands. The latter I have always found excessively nice girls.[17]

And the former? The problem was the connection between nude modelling and sexual impropriety, a problem exacerbated at this period by the change from eighteenth-century acceptance of sex to nineteenth-century abhorrence. It is impossible to pull the female nude model out of the Victorian art world without dealing with the Victorian attitude to sex which clings to her.

Put in its simplest terms, in the second half of the nineteenth century, the nude model became a site for irreconcilable notions about nudity in art (good) and nudity in life (bad). For while the painting of the nude was respected, the unclothed lady who modelled for it was not. In short, the female model represented a clash between the values of art and those of life.

At its strongest this unease led to a desire to bar the nude female model from art schools where unmarried men made up the bulk of the student body. In 1863, the Royal Academician J.R. Herbert told the Royal Commission enquiry that he would

> exclude altogether the nude female model from the Academy because I conceive that Art, the true aim of which is to elevate and divinize, does not require the use of anything which might corrupt him who studies or the person who sits as the model.[18]

Herbert's belief that art should elevate the spectator, and his fear lest the nude female model be corrupted by her work or corrupt the students, add a peculiarly Victorian gloss to the debate.

In his desire to get rid of the female nude model, Herbert was at one with the purity campaigners, that powerful nineteenth-century pressure group whose aim was a sexually unpolluted Britain. Because the female model was the focus of a lot of troubling notions about sex and art and society which in the repressive Victorian climate could find no satisfactory means of coexisting, she became an upsetting member of society for those of a cleansing cast of mind.

In 1885, *Seeking and Saving*, a journal of 'Home, mission and penitentary work', reported the disturbing case of

> a servant girl of over 20 years of age, of irreproachable character and good principles, a communicant [who] consulted her mistress, and the latter consulted her husband, as to what answer the girl should give to an offer of employment as a naked model for male students at a School of Art (not a private studio). The girl had a very perfect figure; the pay per hour was considerable, and she was told that she would have many hours in the day at her own disposal. The girl's wages in her situation were comparatively small; she thought it an opening which would enable her to better support an aged and dying mother, entirely dependent on her, for a year or so, when she could resume her life as a servant. Surely the only safe advice to be given would be 'refuse the offer,' as God's blessing could not be asked on such an occupation.[19]

This story and others like it marked the fact that 1885 was the high tide of a purity campaign aimed at the fine arts whose waves reached as far as the humble nude model. She found herself the subject of several articles in *Seeking and Saving*; she was brought into a correspondence in *The Times* on nudity in art; and was discussed in a widely reported speech which the Royal Academician John Callcott Horsley gave to the Church Congress.

What worried the purity campaigners was the potential

for sexual immorality when a nude woman posed for a male painter. The opposite situation was so dreadful to contemplate that very little was written about it. That it caused the campaigners great distress at a period when female art education was expanding goes without saying, although they were too delicate to give their reasons: 'As regards the supreme reasons against the admission of the female students to the study of the male nude, they cannot be mentioned to a maiden's ears.'[20]

Some ingenious ways of stamping out the female nude model were suggested by *Seeking and Saving*. One solution aimed to reduce the number of models by reducing the number of life classes. The idea was to restrict the life class to those who could prove they possessed the 'high art talent for design, as distinguished from, and in addition to, the power of merely drawing, copying & etc.' It was estimated that this would cut down the number of male students in the life school by eighty per cent and the women students 'to whom the power of designing has been so rarely granted', by ninety-five per cent. Those who remained would be the 'born artists', whose talent would enable them to walk untouched through the lion's den of the life class.

> In proportion to the student's real inspiration for art will be his power of passing scathless through the dangers of the Life School. To him the beauty of female form is no more than the beauty of the male. In each alike his quest is for subtle beauties of proportion, line, equipoise, foreshortening, colour and anatomical learning. But to the student who falls short of this high, purifying, and only admissiable standard, the Life School may be *moral poison*.[21]

The more practical campaigners must have realized that limiting the entrance to the life class in a period of educational expansion was a hopeless cause, so they focused on the model instead. Following a thought process akin to that of the anti-prostitution campaigners, they hoped that by wiping out the model they would wipe out the opportunities for immorality they felt she encouraged. They hit on the idea of presenting the female model as a victim, someone who needed protection from the work's dangers and degradations, and themselves as knights on white chargers who would whisk her away from the profession which caused her so much moral and physical danger.

Not all the strategies to eradicate the nude model were this impractical. Some campaigners tried to raise consciousness on the question of the employment of female nude models. 'An Englishwoman' writing in *Seeking and Saving* was positively Jesuitical in her approach. Would male artists allow their nearest female relations to sit?

> There are many respectable callings no gentleman could wish his wife or daughter to undertake because they are too fatiguing, or on account of the associates to which such callings would expose them. The length of time for which models sit is a matter of arrangement, habit soon renders it easy. Their associates would be those of their own rank in life.[22]

If in spite of this, she asks, an artist still refuses to let his wife or daughter model, how can he justify demanding some other woman to expose herself?

> This is but another form of that principle, long accepted by many — namely that while some women are to receive all possible honour, others are to be condemned to any misuse that may be demanded of them, this latter class being always the poorest, and, therefore, the weakest in the great battle for life; consequently the most likely to be vanquished by men's money — that deadly weapon, constantly employed against woman's modesty.[23]

This argument, which is a product of the alliance that existed in the 1880s between feminism and the purity movement, is still in use today, although exploitation not morality is the banner under which it marches.

Another approach was to get religion on the campaigners' side by presenting modelling's violation of womanly modesty as un-Christian.

> We have been informed by an Artist that he believes many

of them thoroughly respectable, and perfectly modest. It is their profession. But stating the case broadly, is it right for a Christian woman to expose herself unclothed before an Artist for the purpose of earning money? Could one conscientiously tell any modest girl that it was a suitable way for her to gain her living?[24]

Posing without clothes was seen as a first step on a downward path that led to the release of volcanic passions on the part of both artist and model.

> There can be no doubt whatever that persons, male or female, who earn their living by exhibiting their naked or almost naked persons to other men and women, and that for many hours at a time, have adopted as an occupation one that is very dangerous to the models and to the artists — this is more especially true in the case of *private* studios. The natural modesty which is so valuable a protection to purity even when not based on religion, must incur a sad risk of being irremediably tarnished in 'models', male or female, that expose their naked or slightly draped bodies to other persons, whether in a private studio or in a public class.[25]

An admission that it might be impossible to stamp out modelling is implicit in the notion of a writer who wondered whether a version of the night school for models run in connection with the Ladies Art College in Rome might be opened for London's estimated five hundred models. It would be interesting to know more about this school; the article quotes a letter written to its founder which says 'it may be the expiation which Art owes to generations of human beings, who have lent their material gifts to the Painter and the Sculptor, and for whose souls no man has cared'.[26]

The purity campaigners had their supporters among the artists. In summer 1885 a paper, 'Religion and Art', an impressive exercise in fervour and lack of facts, was read by the Royal Academician John Callcott Horsley at a church congress in Portsmouth.

To put the case plainly from a Christian point of view —

> if pictures or statues of naked women are to be executed, living naked women must be employed as models. But where is the justification in God's sight for those who induce women so to ignore their natural modesty, and quench their sense of true shame, as to expose their nakedness before men, and thus destroy all that is pure and lovely in their womanhood?[27]

To illustrate the horror of the work, he told the tale of a fallen woman who hearing money was to be earned from modelling, presented herself at an art school. On learning what was required, she had to be bribed before she would remove her clothes and step on to the model's stage:

> finding herself suddenly under the glare of gaslight naked before forty or fifty students, the poor frightened creature threw up her arms, and with a wild shriek fell fainting on the floor. On recovering she, uttering fearful language, dashed the money on the ground, huddled on her garments, and rushed from the place in a storm of passion, the outcome of the few remains of modesty she still possessed. Ah! if those who talk and write so glibly of the desirability of artists devoting themselves to the representation of the human form only knew a tithe of the degradation enacted before the model is sufficiently hardened to her shameful calling, they would for ever hold their tongues and pens from supporting the practice.[28]

The purity campaigners took their dislike of the female nude model to its logical conclusion by trying to get rid of nude representations in painting and sculpture. This battle took place in the correspondence columns of *The Times*. The first move was made on 20 May 1885, when A British Matron complained about the nude paintings at the Royal Academy and the Grosvenor Gallery. Her grounds were that since nudity was against the law in society, 'the indecent pictures that disgrace our exhibitions' were against the spirit of this law.

Part of the problem, as she saw it, was the embarrassment such pictures caused:

Can one venture to deny that, at an exhibition purporting to be for general edification or entertainment, no picture should find place before which a modest woman may not stand hanging on the arm of father, brother or lover without a burning sense of shame?

Furthermore, people are forced to give only 'timid half glances' to nearby pictures, 'lest it should be supposed the spectator is looking at that which revolts his or her sense of decency'. Concluding by referring to the noble crusade of purity that had been started to check the 'rank profligacy that abounds in our land', she wondered if picture galleries, 'which ought to be sources of innocent and ennobling refinement' should be forbidden to the crusade's members.

She had her supporters. Senex suggested adopting the policy of the Naples Museum and setting a room aside for obscene objects and expanded the topic to include the plight of the artists' models, whom he saw as following an occupation related to, though not as dreadful as, prostitution: 'not, alas! the most pitiable of all, but one too often adopted as the only practicable means of escape from a still worse alternative'.[29] An Englishwoman wrote that no woman likes to contemplate that which tells of the suffering or shame of a less fortunate sister. A member of the Church of England Purity Society feared that the increasing number of life class students of both sexes, for whom 'the inspection of nude representations of the figure is an everyday occurence', would lead to a growth in taste for such exhibitons.[30] Another British Parent compared nude studies with dissection classes.

An artist must learn how to paint flesh as a surgeon must know how to operate upon it. But we don't want the former to turn his training to account by exhibiting 'studies' on the walls of the Royal Academy, that, if they pour in, as they show some signs of doing, in sufficient number, bid fair before long to render that honoured institution about as fitting and agreeable place of recreation for a mixed crowd of the young of both sexes as the dissecting room of a flourishing hospital.[31]

The purity campaigners failed to change the course of art. Victorian painters went on painting nudes, though not as many as the French. A contributer to *The Times* debate suggested the British Matron thank Providence for saving her from being an art-loving Frenchwoman:

> Because at Paris on the walls of this year's Salon, I counted the other day no less than 78 pictures representing whole-length and 38 half-length absolutely nude ladies assisting by their presence to 'break down utterly the lofty standard of purity' a modest woman ought to love.[32]

By the end of the year, the purity campaigners' war against models was losing heart, helped on its way by remarks, both sensible and sharp, in the press. On 24 October 1885, *Punch* published a cartoon of Mr H-rsl-y as 'The Model "British Matron"' looking in horror at the Venus de Medici and exclaiming, 'Oh dear! Oh dear! Who could ha' sat for *that*?' (fig. 12). The modest weekly *The Artist* crushed Horsley's Church Congress speech beneath its heel, stating in an editorial 'Models and Morals' that the study of the nude was linked to the highest kind of art and reproaching Horsley for his bad taste in attacking models, 'a class of workers on behalf of art, whose services, though comparatively humble, are none the less indispensable'. And it counteracted Horsley's slight on the model's respectability by pointing out that 'the physical beauties, upon which those persons who sit to artists depend for their employment are just those which rapidly deteriorate and disappear if any but a moral code of life is pursued'.[33]

But where the purity campaigners really hung themselves was in their nude model-prostitute comparison. For prostitute implied a client — in this case, a painter, a member of a respected profession. Sensing failure, the purity campaigners suggested barmaids as a new cause in 1886: 'Their life is one of great temptation, and their profession isolates them from most parochial agencies', meaning, the next sentence reveals, that social workers were not comfortable entering public houses.[34]

Despite the failure of this particular round in the purity campaign, Victorian unease over the problem of the female model remained. The purity campaigners may have been moralists from the lunatic fringe but it has to be recognized that while they were the ones who shouted longest and loudest, their concerns were of interest to more temperate Victorians. However much sophisticated Victorians chanted the mantra that models were the sexless handmaidens of art, deep in their hearts they knew that they were blocking out some pertinent questions about sex, women and art in their society. The issue was a sufficiently disturbing one at this period to be treated by poets and novelists.

In *The Marble Faun* (1859), a novel of artistic life in Rome by the American Nathaniel Hawthorne, the artist Miriam talks of nude sculpture as an art form that has 'wrought itself out':

Every young sculptor seems to think that he must give the world some specimen of indecorous womanhood, and call it Eve, Venus, a Nymph, or any name that may apologise for a lack of decent clothing. I am weary, even more than I am ashamed, of seeing such things. Now-a-days people are as good as born in their clothes, and there is practically not a nude human being in existence. An artist, therefore, — as you must candidly confess, — cannot sculpture nudity with a pure heart, if only because he is compelled to steal guilty glimpses at hired models. The marble inevitably loses its chastity under such circumstances. An old Greek sculptor, no doubt, found his models in the open sunshine, and among pure and princely maidens, and thus the nude statues of antiquity are as modest as violets, and sufficiently draped in their own beauty.[35]

Robert Browning published a short poem, 'The Lady and the Painter', in defence of nude modelling. The grand and fashionable Lady Blanche expresses her disapproval of the artist having a nude model sit for him. In retaliation the artist points to the wild bird wings on Lady Blanche's hat: she, he says, is a murderess of God's beings while the nude model is helping him to praise 'God's surpassing good' by posing for him. Lady Blanche's arguments have already been met with from the pens of the purity campaigners:

> To help Art-Study, — for some dole
> Of certain wretched shillings, — you
> Induce a woman — virgin too —
> To strip and stand stark-naked?

To which the artist replies that Lady Blanche's bird wings disgust him more than

> Did you strip off those spoils you wear,
> And stand — for thanks, not shillings — bare,
> To help Art like my model there.

Victorian artists reveal a great deal about the low status of the female nude model through the way they write about her in their reminiscences. Their doubts about the morality of the model emerge most strongly when they take the greatest pains to deny them. Mrs E.M. Ward informed the readers of her *Reminiscences* that 'It is interesting too, to note that models who sit for the figure are, as a rule, the most moral!'[36] One wonders how she knew and why she felt it necessary to make the claim. 'I have known numbers of *perfectly respectable* women who have sat constantly and habitually for the nude', wrote Frith, whose remarks are echoed by other writers at this period. He continues:

> and even if it were unfortunately otherwise, we painters could not do without them. Many men draw every figure naked in their compositions before they clothe them . . . Then, again, if the nude female figure had always been denied to artists, such statues as the Venus of Milo — the delight and wonder of the world — could not have been executed. Numbers of great works of the old and modern masters would never have seen the light, and generations of their worshippers would have been deprived of exquisite pleasure and untold improvement.[37]

Sometimes the model is presented as suffering in some way, as if the reader's judgement can be organized like scales — immorality in one pan balanced by suffering in the other. A cliché of nude model descriptions by the artists who employ them is their 'brutal' husbands. Frith always presents the female nude model pathetically, seeing tears falling down the face of the life class model at the Academy, even though her pose was an easy one, so that, he assures us, she could not have been in pain. Later he learned that she had been forced to model — that is, that she was a Good Girl:

> 'I did it,' said she, 'to prevent my father going to prison. He owed three pounds ten, and if he couldn't have paid it by that Saturday night, he was to be arrested. The Academy paid me three guineas for the week, and saved him. I never sat that way before, and I never will again:' and I believe she never did.[38]

It is revealing of his acceptance of the nude model's low status that when he later tells of this woman's successful marriage he can barely keep the incredulity out of his voice.

It is evident from their need to defend her that artists found their dependence on the nude female model an embarrassment. By representing life nudity before it become art nudity, she was the artists' Achilles' heel.

The female nude model occupied a pivotal position at this period. On one side she was connected to life and inherited all the assumptions of sexuality and immorality that accompanied working in the nude for money. On the other side she was connected to art and heir to notions of purity, beauty and the strain of thought that saw painting as a manifestation of the divine, which still had adherents in the nineteenth century. It was the artist's job to reconcile the two sides, to transform the naked female model into an artistic nude. In her original aspect she was a necessary evil, the shameful and disturbing Victorian body which had to be purified of its sexual connotations before it could be framed in gilt and admired by cultivated Victorians.

For nineteenth-century artists convinced of their calling to elevate, the problem of the nude model's relationship to sex must have seemed as high as Everest. Firmly on the side of conventional morality, dedicated to proving their fitness as respectable members of society, their need to draw from undressed women was the weak link in their respectable front.

In society, sex and pure women had nothing in common, yet in art nude women were expected to be the vessels of inspiring ideas. Perhaps it was a sign that this contradiction was sensed that so many late Victorian artists painted the Pygmalion and Galatea myth in which Pygmalion, legendary king of Cyprus, falls in love with an ivory statue which Aphrodite obligingly brings to life. Academic artists in many countries whose professional reputation was invested in being as respectable as possible, were drawn to this subject, among them the Frenchman Gérôme, one of whose versions of the myth hangs in New York's Metropolitan Museum. In England its most famous exponent is Burne-Jones who in a series of four paintings in Birmingham Art Gallery, done between 1869 and 1879, shows the artist carving, the statue completed, the statue coming to life and the artist embracing her. The titles are, *The Heart Desires, The Hand Refrains, The Godhead Fires, The Soul Attains* (fig. 9).

Can this myth in which the ideal takes on flesh be seen as a wishful solution to the male Victorian artist's problem of the embarrassing nude female model? In a prudish climate one can hardly blame Burne-Jones for envisaging an artist's studio in which the nude model has been replaced by a beautiful nude woman born untainted from a work of art.

Notes

1 Peter Leslie, ed. *The Letters of John Constable* (London, 1931), pp. 164-5.
2 Nikolaus Pevsner, *Academies of Art Past and Present* (Cambridge University Press, 1940) p. 66.
3 Giorgio Vasari, *Lives of the Artists* (Penguin, 1979), p. 449.
4 Ibid., p. 444.
5 Ibid., p. 455.
6 Ibid., pp. 316-17.
7 Ibid., p. 423.
8 Ralph N. Wornum, ed., *Lectures on Painting by the Royal Academicians Barry, Opie and Fuseli* (London, 1848), pp. 251-2.
9 Francis Haskell and Nicholas Penny, *Taste and the Antique* (Yale University Press, 1981), p. 221.
10 'Memoirs of the Late Charles Townley Esq.', *The General Chronicle*

and Literary Magazine, May, 1812.

11 John Galt, *The Life, Studies and Works of Benjamin West, Esq.* (London, 1820), part 2, p. 101.

12 Joseph Baretti, *A Guide Through the Royal Academy* (London, 1781), p. 32.

13 *Report of the Commissioners on the Present Position of the Royal Academy in Relation to the Fine Arts with Minutes of Evidence, Appendix and Index and Observations of Members of The Academy 1863-4* (Irish University Press, 1970), para. 1524.

14 Edward J. Poynter, *Ten Lectures on Art* (London, 1879), Lecture 3, pp. 109-10.

15 William T. Whitley, *Artists and Their Friends in England* (2 vols., London, Medici Society, 1978), vol. 1, p. 17.

16 Edward Edwards, *Anecdotes of Painters* (London, 1808), p. x.

17 Weedon Grossmith, *From Studio to Stage* (London, 1913), p. 42.

18 *Position of the Royal Academy in Relation to the Fine Arts*, para. 4853.

19 *Seeking and Saving*, February 1885, p. 34.

20 Ibid., p. 34.

21 Ibid., pp. 35-6.

22 Ibid., March 1885, pp. 59-60.

23 Ibid., p. 60.

24 Ibid., July 1885, p. 6.

25 Ibid., February 1885, p. 31.

26 Ibid., July 1885, p. 6.

27 Ibid., January 1886, p. 64.

28 Ibid., pp. 64-5.

29 *The Times*, 22 May 1885.

30 Ibid., 23 May 1885.

31 Ibid., 25 May 1885.

32 Ibid., 23 May 1885.

33 *The Artist*, 2 November 1885.

34 *Seeking and Saving*, October 1886.

35 Nathaniel Hawthorne, *The Marble Faun* (Ohio, 1968), ch. 14.

36 Mrs E.M. Ward, *Reminiscences* (London, 1911), p. 220.

37 W.P. Frith, *My Autobiography and Reminiscences* (3 vols., London, 1903), vol. 1, pp. 59-60.

38 Ibid., p. 59.

5
Bohemia

In the middle of the nineteenth century Henry Murger chronicled the existence in Paris of an anarchic artistic community in which the model figured as the artist's partner in crime. Its name was Bohemia. Bohemia was the place the French gave their artists where they could live according to their own rules. Although its concept of morality was different from that of the bourgeois Parisian world, it is a measure of its strength that Parisian society decided to accommodate it. Bohemia existed for about one hundred years. Its life span, which began with Courbet and ended when Picasso and Matisse were old men, coincided with the rise and fall of the School of Paris. And like the paintings of the Paris School, it proved to be an exportable and influential commodity.

Bohemia took forty years to reach England, but when it arrived it improved the status of the artist's model. The female artist's model, that is. The male model, though in constant employment in art schools until the middle of the twentieth century, fell a victim to the myth of Bohemia as inhabited by lusty male creative artists and their mistress-models.

It is Bohemia that stamped the consciousness of art as a male activity on an age which saw the introduction of women into art schools. It is Bohemia that turned models into women. It is Bohemia's determination to see all models as glamorous inhabitants of an exciting artistic community that has pushed the contrary evidence into an attic from which it is only now beginning to emerge. Above all it is Bohemia that brought the English artist-model relationship out of its nineteenth-century secrecy by giving it an exciting image and an acceptable context in which to thrive. Once artists stopped aspiring to a bourgeois existence and flaunted their own way of life before bourgeois eyes, the artist-model relationship had to be accepted.

It was Henry Murger in *Scènes de la vie de bohème*, published as short stories from 1845 and in book form in 1851, who formulated the idea of an artistic country with a set of laws and values that corresponded to, yet differed from, those of the greater, straighter world which surrounded it. Without being in any way salacious (Mimi's mention of posing to an artist for the head and hand is enough to fill Rodolphe with jealousy), Murger's tales of his group of artists — all male of course — presented to the public an attractive alternative world of poverty and creativity peopled with artists and their mistresses whose pleasures went unpunished. The fact that men and women lived together in Bohemian 'marriage' as Murger called it, was a fact of their way of life. Murger's book mapped out Bohemia and described its customs for the bourgeois in France to read, in much the same spirit no doubt as they were already swallowing Eugène Sue's tales of slum life.

In his preface, Murger wrote that Bohemia could only exist in Paris, and it is certainly true that it did not take root in England until the translation of the book into English in 1887 introduced Murger's concept to this country. In the mid nineteenth century, when Murger's short stories were published in France, no parallel Bohemia existed in England. The image Victorian artists desired was one of deepest respectability, convincing proof of the professional status they prized so much. English artists felt with justification that an irregular lifestyle would do them nothing but harm if news of it reached the picture-buying public. Holman Hunt's terror lest his family or readers guess he was the prototype of the artist in 'Calmuck' makes that clear. The lack of an English Murger to celebrate life and love among the artists meant that even when artists went in for such things, which certain Pre-Raphaelites most definitely did, they did not wish the news to leak out of their immediate circle.

But though England had no Bohemia on French lines, it did have a version of its own. English Bohemia lacked the women to live with and the poverty that encouraged its French inhabitants to such picturesque criminal acts as moonlight flits. But it possessed some of the necessary ingredients in the shape of artists, intellectuals and a tendency to feel superior to polite society. There are two forms of English Bohemia in the nineteenth century. One is the state of being outside the social conventions in some way. The other resembles a men's club.

Thackeray is the great describer of the first. At the start of the 1860s in a gently comic piece of writing in *The Adventures of Philip*, Thackeray equates Bohemianism with slipping off one's tight society shoes as the heir and hero leaves the home of his love for the house of his friends:

> From long residence in Bohemia, and fatal love of bachelor ease and habits, Master Philip's pure tastes were so destroyed, and his manners so perverted, that he was actually indifferent to the pleasures of the refined home we have just been describing;... At the house whither he is now going, he and the cigar are always welcome. There is no need of munching orange chips, or chewing scented pills, or flinging your weed away half a mile before you reach Thornhaugh street — the low vulgar place.[1]

Although *Philip* is set in the 1830s, the concept of Bohemia as outside polite society, a place where tobacco and drink and conversation could be freely enjoyed, was current when Thackeray wrote the book. It still had life twenty years later when in 1881 *Punch* commented on the newspapers' practice of listing visitors to watering places. These are good places to avoid, says *Punch*, for those who 'want to Bohemianise a bit, and to get away, for a while at least, from the humbug of our veneered town life'.[2]

Thackeray also expresses Bohemianism as being outside conventional society by using an early French meaning of the word as vagabond, a meaning which developed from the equation of Bohemia with the gypsies who were thought to stem from there. In 1848, three years after Murger first used Bohemian to describe the lifestyle of his group of artists, Thackeray used it in connection with Becky Sharp's racketings round the Europe of the 1820s, one of a band of raffish drinkers and brawlers.

> So our little wanderer went about, setting up her tent in various cities of Europe as restless as Ulysses or Bamfylde Moore Carew. Her taste for disrespectability grew more and more remarkable. She would become a perfect Bohemian ere long, herding with people whom it would make your hair stand on end to meet.[3]

Becky's life with its 'alternations of splendour and misery' has the element of unconventionality familiar from Murger's writings. But whereas Murger has anchored his Bohemians in a Parisian framework, Thackeray clings to the word's gypsy connotations. Carew became the king of the gypsies in the eighteenth century.

The equating of Bohemianism with gypsies continued for a long time in England. Maggie Andrews, adopted daughter of Sir William and Lady Hewitt and heroine of *Bohemian Blood* (1910) by Lester Lurgan, learns of her gypsy heritage through her 'finely statuesque' gypsy uncle, whom we first meet as he models for an artist. 'The daughter of a wandering vagrant! Did it not explain the untameable Bohemianism of her nature? That baffling against restraint, the love of freedom, of wandering restlessness under the canopy of heaven?'[4] The link between gypsies and Bohemianism has its most flamboyant manifestation about this time in the Romany caravan which Augustus John lived in from 1905 with his wife, mistress and children.

The other form taken by English Bohemia was that of the men's club. Unlike Murger's characters who live a permanent life of love and art in a place called Bohemia, the more moderate English tended to don their Bohemianism periodically, meeting once a week to discuss artistic and intellectual matters.

This Bohemia of artists and intellectuals came in first and second class. Second class catered for the non-establishment men who met over a meal in taverns in Covent Garden or the Strand. (The home of the eighteenth-century drawing schools had kept its artistic connections.) Joseph Hatton recalls in 'Glimpses of Bohemia' in the Christmas 1893 number of *The Bohemian* that 'the Bohemia to which I was introduced was, I think, the Savage Club, during one of its migratory phases'. Henry Stacey Marks remembers a small club in the 1850s called The Circle made up of members of all the arts: 'We were Bohemian and nomad. Having no settled habitation, we met at rooms in taverns, generally in the neighbourhood of Covent Garden.'[5]

First-class Bohemia was based in the St John's Wood and Kensington homes of the artistic rich, where successful intellectuals, artists and wives — occasionally unaccompanied by husbands — could converse on mutually agreeable subjects. In his novel *The Queen of Bohemia* published in 1877, Joseph Hatton tells the tale of Mrs Toynbee, the Queen of the title, rich, beautiful and twice widowed, who runs a weekly salon in St John's Wood. One of her glittering guest lists includes a great Italian composer, a prima donna, a successful artist, a barrister's beautiful wife and 'Winwood Masters, the traveller and his wife, whom King Penniwenky wanted to buy for a gingham umbrella.' Mrs Toynbee's receptions are a far cry from Stacey Marks's tavern: 'There is a special counter for American drinks, introduced for the first time on this occasion, and presided over by a smart New York barman, who is very popular with the men.'[6]

Despite Hatton's unaccompanied and desirable wives, women are rare visitors to either of the English Bohemias. Towards the end of the century several references are made to the ease of male-female relationships in Bohemian England, but this seems to have been more wishful thinking than reality: 'Our London Bohemia . . . is the world of free men and tolerant, toilers in the broad fields of art, where both sexes meet without masks, and talk without affectation', wrote Hatton in *The Bohemian* in 1893. But he does not really believe it, and more convincing is his nostalgic view of Bohemia in the magazine's January 1894 issue as strictly masculine territory:

There are still, no doubt, Bohemians, in plenty, men who live their own lives and have no fear of Mrs. Grundy, men who don't turn up their trousers except when it rains, men who have no small talk for evening parties and who do not crowd the staircases of Mayfair on summer after-noons, men who take life earnestly and live naturally and give God thanks for the sun that grows tobacco and ripens the vine of hop and grape; but the landmarks of Bohemia are changed, the outposts, settlements and roof-trees of my youth, are no more.

Sex is as rare as women in English Bohemia. None of the articles or novels about Bohemia display an equivalent to the 'marriages' that stud Murger's *Vie de bohème*. The only hint that sexual irregularity might be a part of Bohemianism comes in Henry James's novel *The Europeans*, published in London in 1878. As the amateur painter Felix asks Mr Wentworth for his daughter's hand he admits 'I have been a Bohemian — yes; but in Bohemia I always passed for a gentleman ... It was the liberty I liked, but not the opportunities! My sins were all peccadilloes; I always respected my neighbour's property — my neighbour's wife.'[7] But then Felix had been educated on the Continent and his American creator was nothing if not sophisticated in his social attitudes.

The change from English to French-style Bohemia was marked by the first English translation of Murger's book in 1887 under the title *The Bohemians of the Latin Quarter*. This was followed in 1892 by Fergus Hume's *When I Lived in Bohemia*, a book of short stories which the author envisaged as an English version of Murger's *Vie de bohème* without the 'charming immoralities', as Hume felt the 'English public would have blushed at the vagaries of Mademoiselle Mimi'.[8] In 1894 came George du Maurier's *Trilby* with its account of love among the English artists in mid-century Paris. In 1907 Arthur Ransome's *Bohemia in London*, with its claim that London's Bohemia could stand next to the French version without undue humiliation, marked Bohemia's debut into non-fiction, although occasional articles on the subject had been appearing since the early 1890s.

For a few years at the end of the eighties and the start of the nineties, the outgoing English Bohemia and the incoming French Bohemia existed side by side in England. Their contrasting styles are symbolised by two magazines, both called *The Bohemian* but one representing the old and one the new Bohemia.

The Bohemian of 1887 was a sober affair, a sparsely

illustrated political, literary and critical journal. Although it was aimed at 'all the tribes of Bohemia', a borrowing of Murger's formulation of the 'races, classes and subdivisions' of Bohemia, it was clearly after the respectable Stacey Marks type of Bohemian who worked hard and limited his Bohemian indulgences to a weekly tavern chat. Dedicated to upgrading the image of Bohemianism, the magazine threw the popular image of the Bohemian as an 'idle ne'er do well, possessing some artistic taste, combined with a predilection for tobacco and strong drink and an extraordinary talent for avoiding his creditors' into the wastebasket. 'The true Bohemian,' it claimed, 'is primarily an artist, generally a hard working one, who has to depend upon his ability for his livelihood by his art, music, painting, the drama or any other.'[9] The assumption that Bohemians were well-behaved members of the community with similar interests to non-Bohemians is reflected in the contents, which contained an 'Eminent Bohemians' series, chess problems and a parliamentary column called 'the Bohemian Behind the Speaker's Chair'. The 'Bohemian Talk' column claimed the explorer H.M. Stanley as a 'worthy Bohemian' after he had been given the freedom of the City of London.

The Bohemian founded in 1893 was a much jollier affair, a monthly review of literature, drama and art edited by S.L. Bensusan, which by 1895 had evolved into a racy illustrated journal with an interest in the music-halls and the tag 'An Unconventional Magazine' below the masthead. The fact that when *The Bohemian* b. 1887 interviewed an actress it meant Ellen Terry, and the fact that when *The Bohemian* b. 1893 interviewed one it meant a lady of the chorus, illustrates the difference between the two.

Contrasting articles about artists' models reveal the replacement of the nineteenth century's patronizing attitude towards them with a brand new interest in their work. *Bohemian 1* of 2 April 1887, describes a male model who was a bootblack and errand boy until his discovery by a figure painter, a model during his teens and twenties and a frame-maker after marriage. The tone is arch and reference is made to the model's cockney origins:

I was told with great pride by the young fellow that

Mr. Three Stars 'painted all his figures from him, men, women and children; not cats and dogs, for Mr. Three Stars does not paint cats and dogs, but little lambs often'.

Bohemian 2 of Christmas 1893 takes an informative line, discussing pay and conditions of work, playing down the class element and also, a significant change, concentrating on female models. However, even advanced English Bohemians knew where to draw the line, as Charles D. Steele's short story, 'A Mad Marriage', in the December 1895 *Bohemian* illustrates. Learning on his wedding night that his French bride, an ex-waitress in a Bohemian cafe, has another man's name tattooed on her arm, the horrified English artist

> staggered out of doors; the rain was falling now in torrents. His brain reeled. There was another peel of thunder and a lurid flash of lightening. He looked back again and yet again at the couch on which the beautiful girl who had ruined his life was lying.

And he went off and drowned himself in the raging sea.

By the mid nineties the idea of Bohemia was taking hold of the popular fancy. According to *The Bohemian* of August 1895 a chorus in Owen Hall's musical comedy *An Artist's Model* was 'Gay Bohemi-ah . . . with the accent on the Ah!' The word, reported the magazine, crops up continually in contemporary literature, adding facetiously that 'now the ladies of Bootle have elected to form a Bohemian Cycling Club'.

It was not chance that the reference to Bohemia occurred in a play called *An Artist's Model*, for one form the fashion for Bohemia took was an interest in the female model who was seen as Bohemia's most fascinating inhabitant. In 1894, a South London music-hall called the Washington ran a sketch called 'An Artist's Model or Eve Before the Fall', the theatrical weekly *The Era* commenting that Miss Louise Hastings who played Nellie Knowall the model was 'what Mr. Mantalini would have called "a damned fine woman" '.

In 1895, a year after its publication, Du Maurier's novel *Trilby* was staged at London's Haymarket Theatre with Dorothea Baird as the model Trilby and Beerbohm Tree as

Svengali, and this fanned the flames of interest in the artist's model. In November, *Punch* carried a cartoon about the Trilby mania and in December *The Bohemian* remarked on the Trilby boom, mentioning that half a dozen songs on the subject were being sung on the halls. Productions already running were quick to add a topical Trilby reference. A song called 'Trilby' was inserted into a revival of *An Artist's Model*. 'A Trilby Triflet' was introduced into the second act of *Gentleman Joe*, a burlesque of Baird and Tree's performances in the Haymarket play, and 'A Modern Trilby' was produced at the Opera Comique by Nelly Farren. The interest the theatre took in the model was a two-way affair, since many of Britain's avant-garde artists were fascinated by music-hall performers: Whistler, Wilson Steer and Sickert all painted female artistes in the eighties and nineties.

The interest in the model as a theatrical character continued up to the First World War. In 1910 the Garrick Theatre put on *Dame Nature*, a toned-down version of a French play known as *La Femme Nue*. America shared the interest in model heroines. *An Artist's Model* toured there in 1896, and in 1912 a play called *The Model* by Augustus Thomas opened at the Harris Theatre in New York in which Louise Lange, the model of the title, is referred to as a 'Bohemian person'.

This play is interesting for its picture of the artist-model relationship on the turn from socially unacceptable to socially acceptable. The new way is represented by the artist-hero Duncan Coverly's desire to marry his model, the old way by the Frenchman Bergeret whose view of the unsuitability of artist-model marriages is expressed in an irresistible mixture of continental worldliness and conservative wisdom. Bergeret believes that models make good mistresses but bad wives: 'To have the woman that you call your wife denied on every side — and the inexorable social world against her? To dine always alone with her. To be invited only where gentlemen convene and not ladies.' Marrying a model can only lead to professional suicide:

The honeymoon? — over too — the young couple return. Here? Very good for breakfast, good for a few painter friends who drop in — the great patrons then? The people

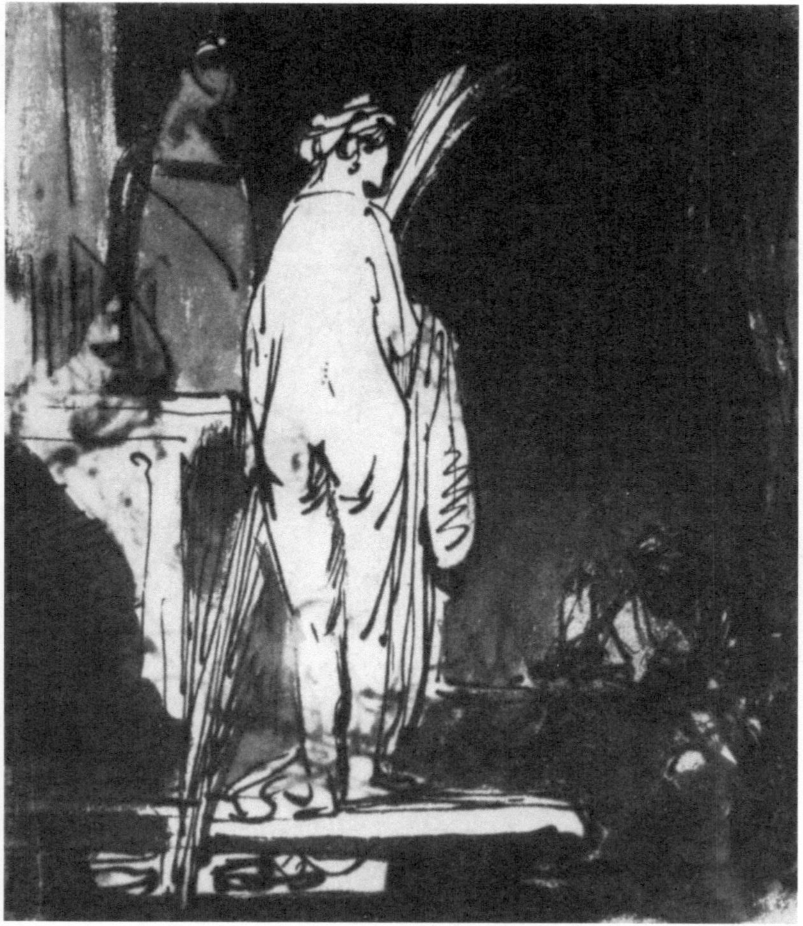

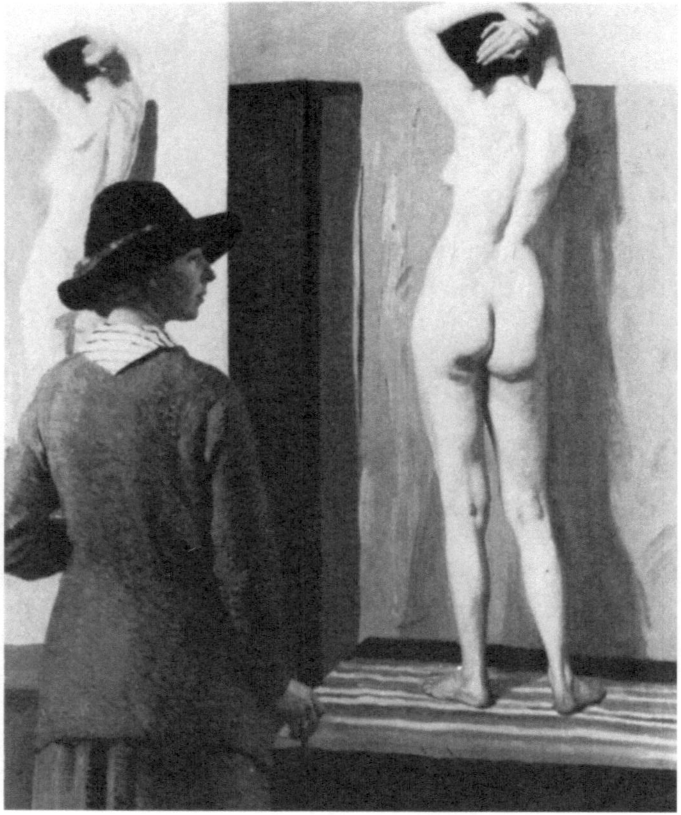

1 (*left*) Rembrant, *The Artist Drawing from a Model*, c. 1639
2 (*above*) Dame Laura Knight, *Self-portrait*, 1913

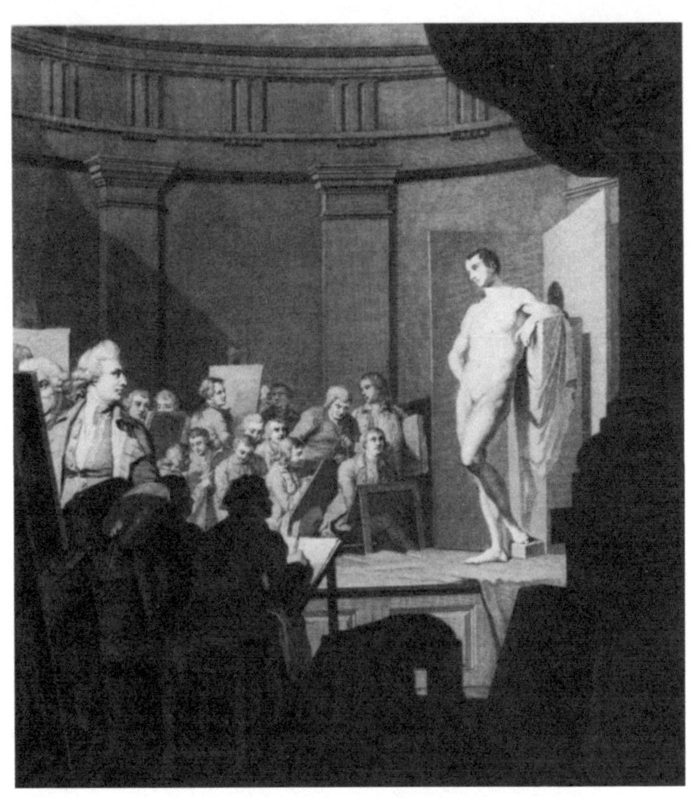

3 Engraving by Simon Ravenet after a picture by John Hamilton Mortimer, published 1771

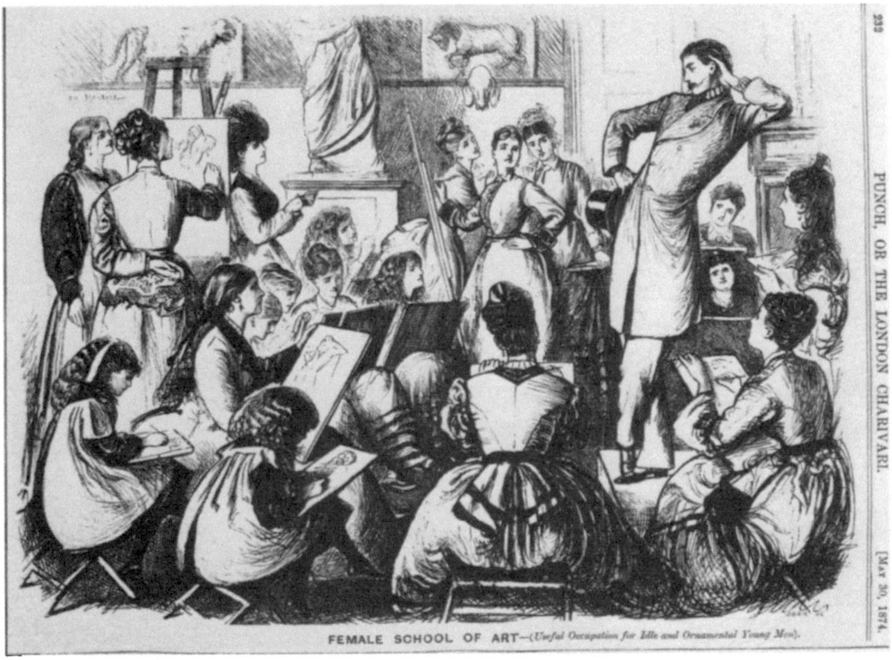

4 *Punch*, 30 May 1874

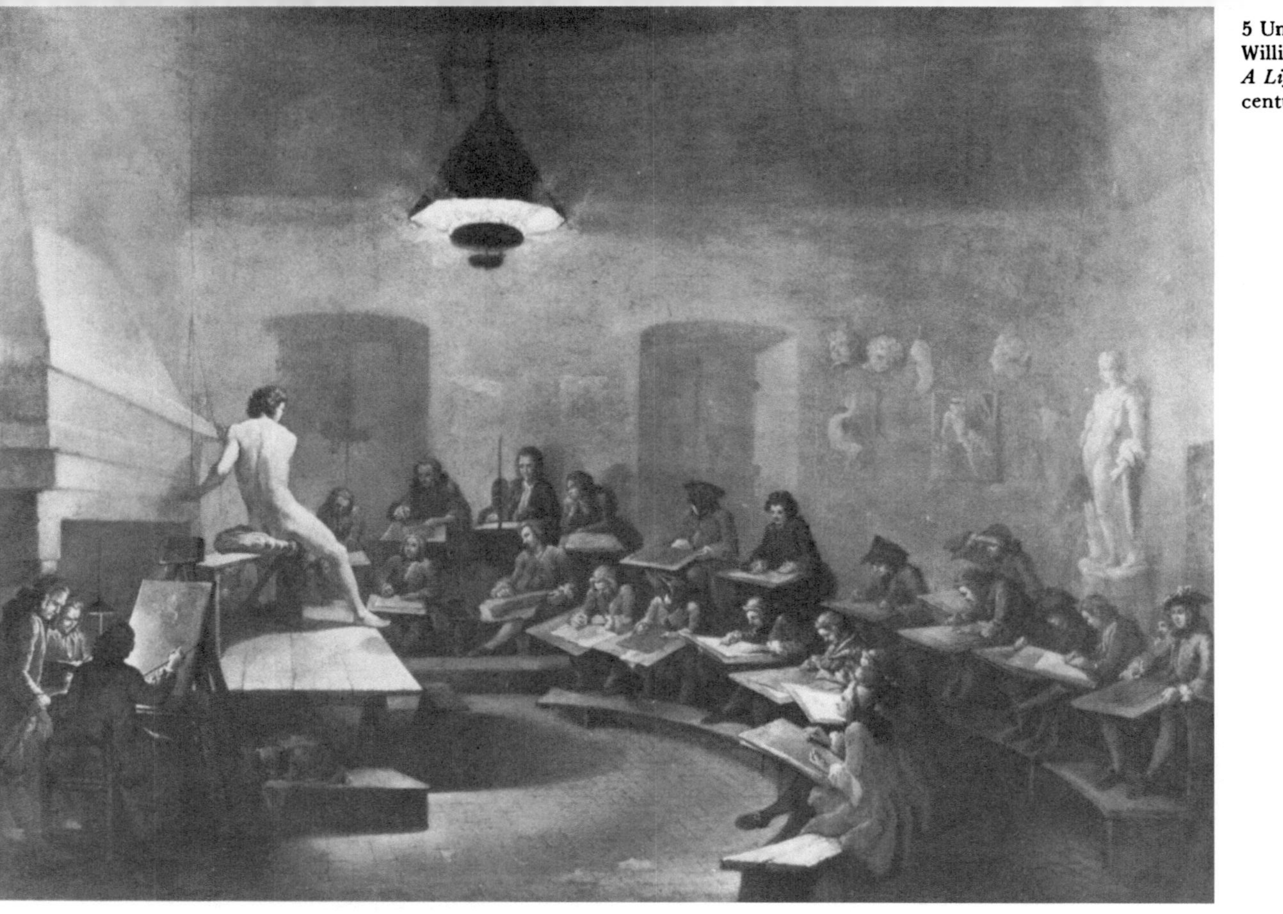

5 Unknown artist,
William Hogarth *attr.*,
A Life School, 18th
century

6 Thomas Rowlandson, *Lady H . . . . . 's (Hamilton's) Attitudes,* c. 1800

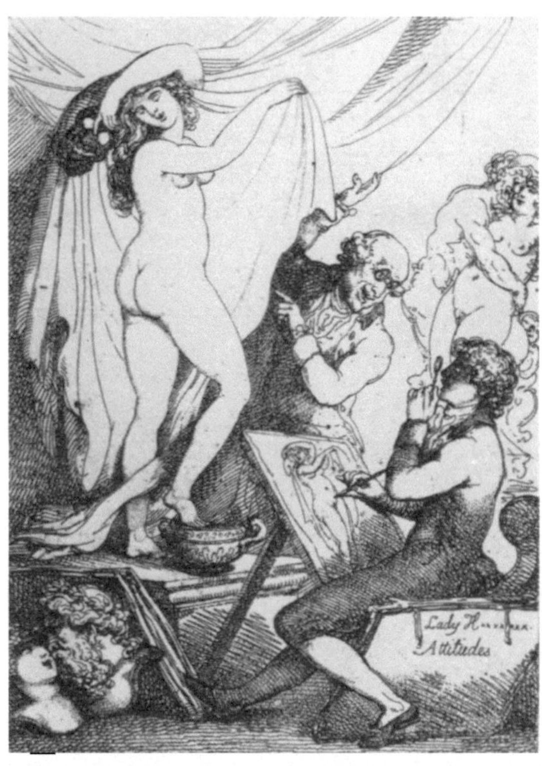

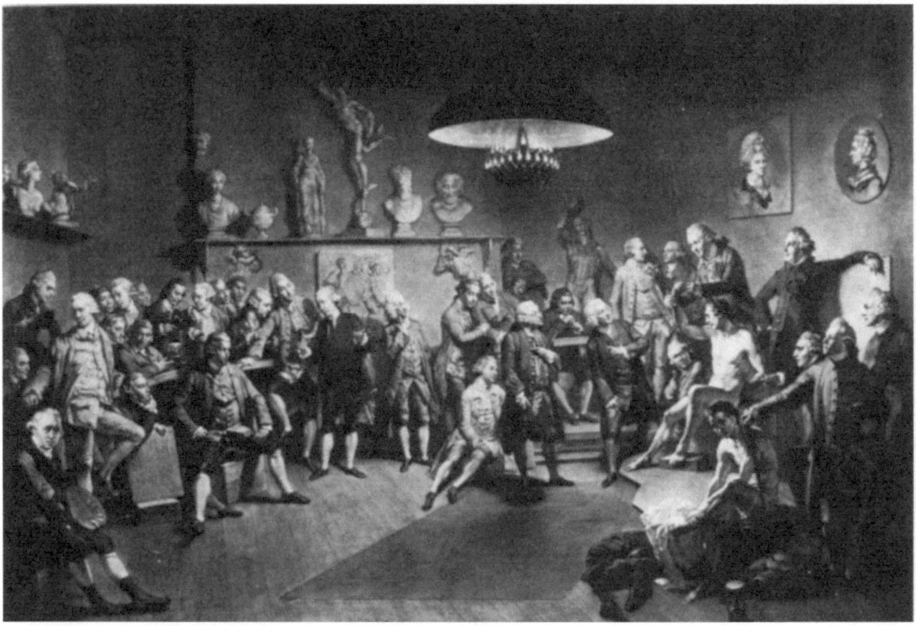

7 J. Saunders, *Royal Academicians,* 1773, after the painting by J. Zoffany, *The Academicians of the Royal Academy,* 1771-2

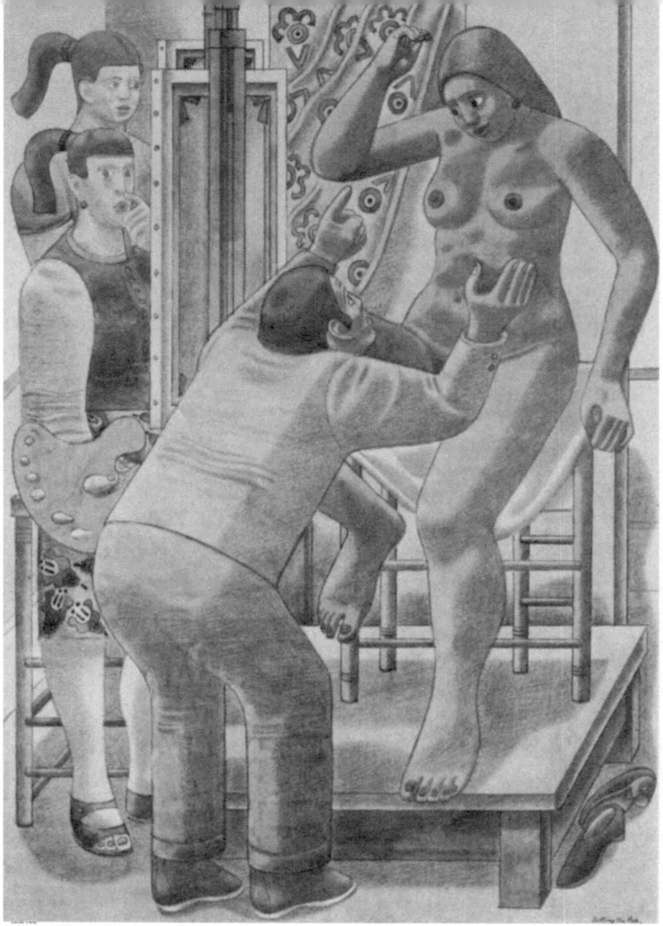

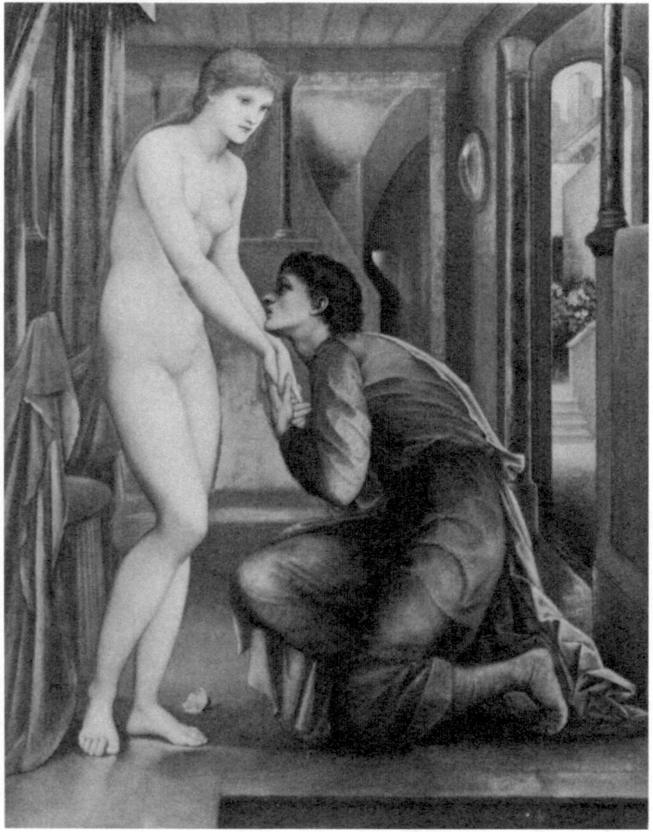

8 (*left*) William Roberts, *Setting the Pose*, 1952
9 (*above*) Edward Burne-Jones, *Pygmalion and Galatea: The Soul Attains*, 1869-79

BALLAD OF THE PROFESSIONAL MODEL.

So there you are, old patriarch,
  I sat for in the spring—
If you 'll permit me to remark,
  As like as anything!

But now you 're in a gorgeous dress,
  And in a big gold frame;
The passers stare, but hardly guess
  We are the very same.

Also, you 're looking twice as fresh
  As I am, you 'll agree—
You 've got more colour and more flesh,
  Which ain't as it should be.

You know you 'd never have been there
  Without me, to enjoy
These many blessings—can't we share
  And share alike, old boy.

248   PUNCH, OR THE LONDON CHARIVARI.   [DECEMBER 12, 1874.

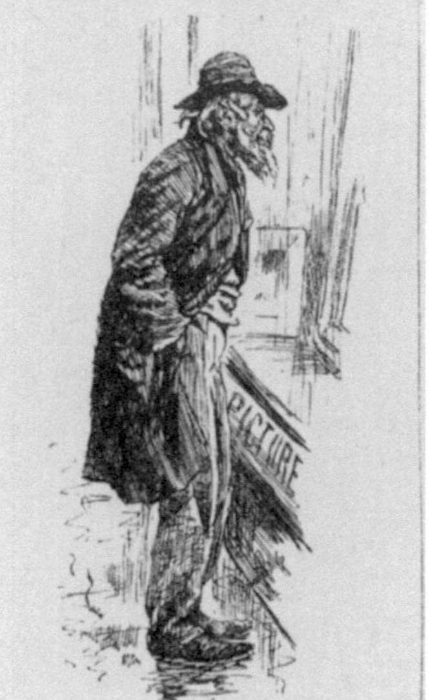

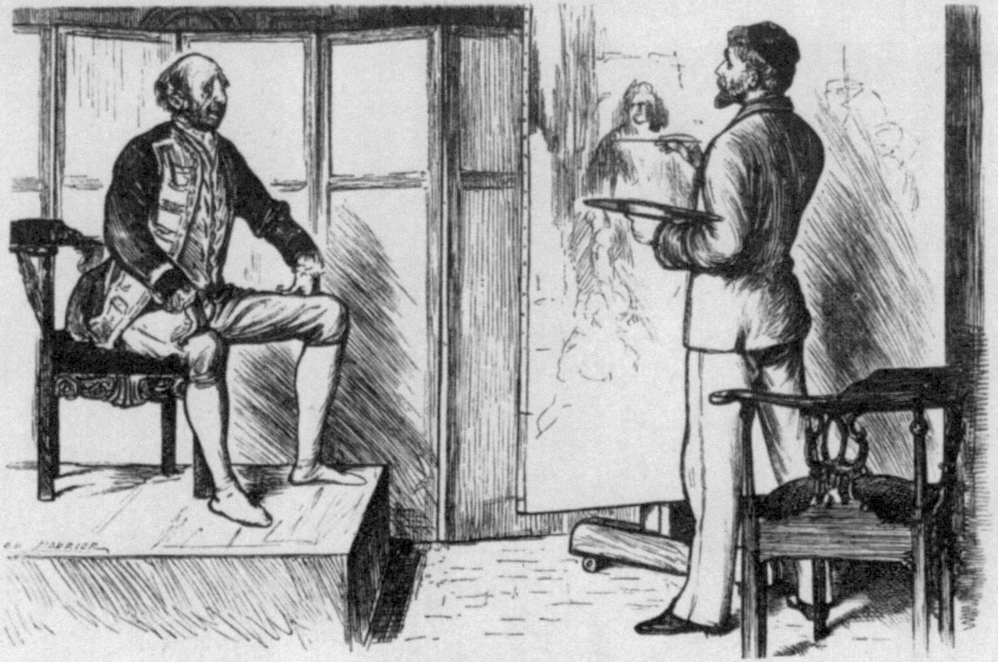

BROTHERS IN ART.

Playful R.A. (to his Model, who has been expatiating on the dignity of the Working Man). "I AM PLEASED TO PERCEIVE, JAKES, THAT YOU ARE CONTENT WITH YOUR HUMBLE CONDITION, AND DO NOT ENVY THE LOT OF THE SUPERIOR CLASSES!"

Jakes. "HENVY 'EM! WHY, BLESS YER, THEM AS BELONGS TO THEM CLASSES AS YOU ALLUDES TO AIN'T 'ALF SO MUCH TO BE HENVIED AS THEM AS BELONGS TO THE CLASS AS ME AND YOU BELONGS TO."

10 (*left*) *Punch*, 27 January 1894

11 (*above*) *Punch*, 12 December 1874

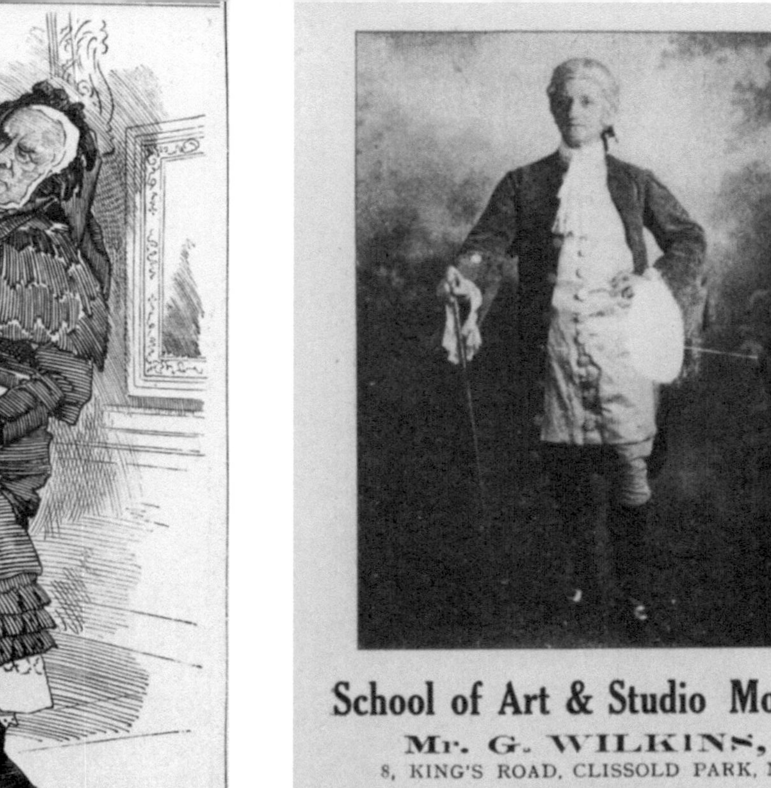

12 (*left*) *Punch*, 24 October 1885

13 (*above*) *The Art Chronicle*, 11 December 1909

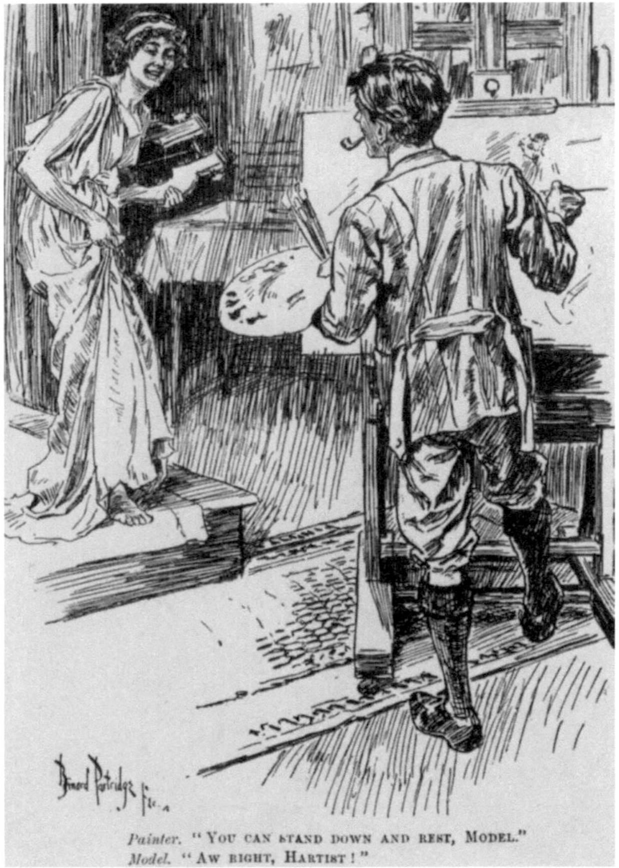

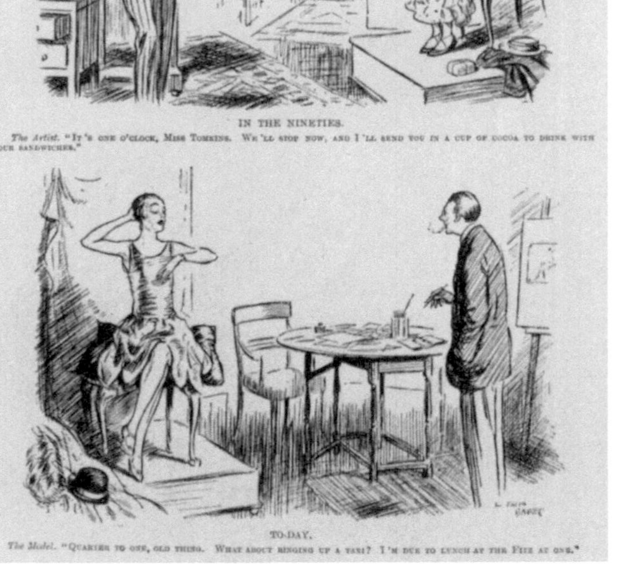

14 *Punch*, 10 October 1900

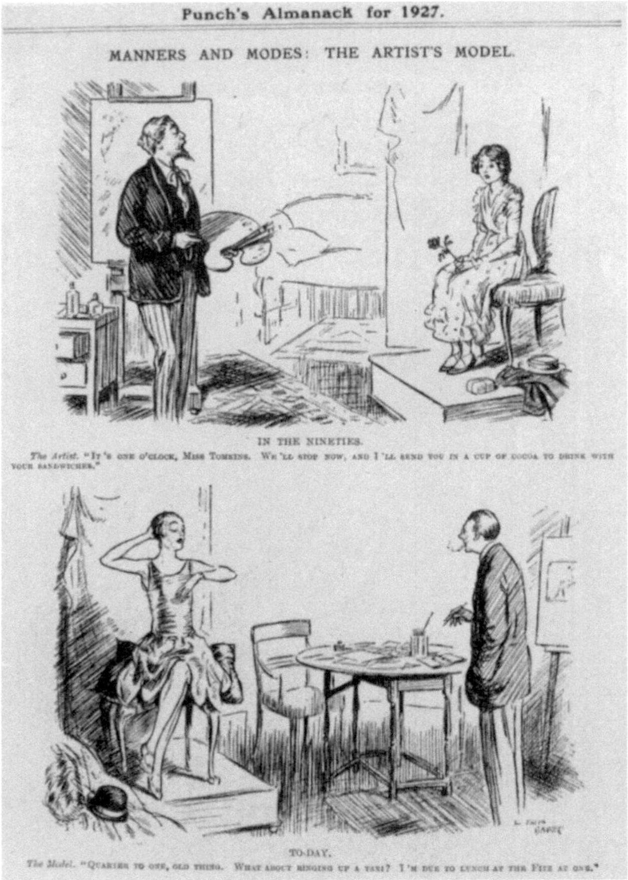

15 *Punch*, *Almanack for 1927*, 1 November 1926

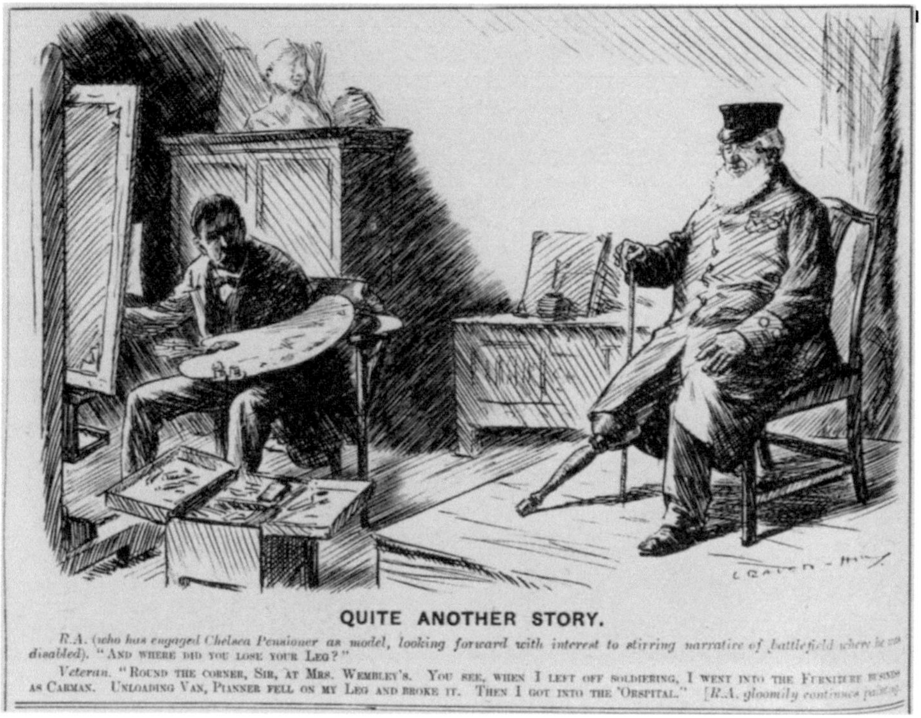

16 *Punch*, 27 April 1904

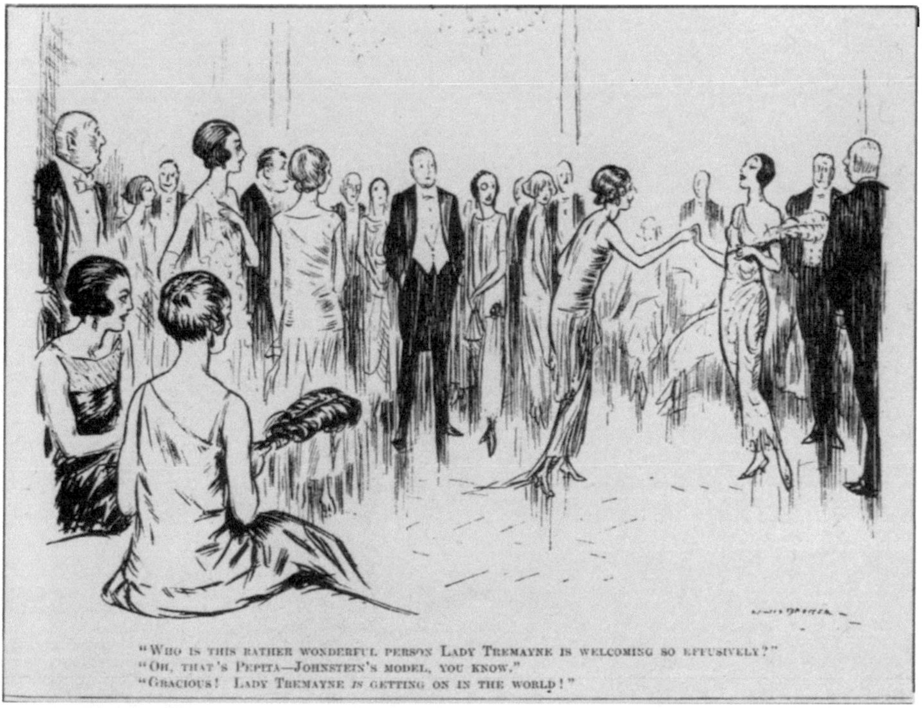

17 *Punch*, 21 May 1924

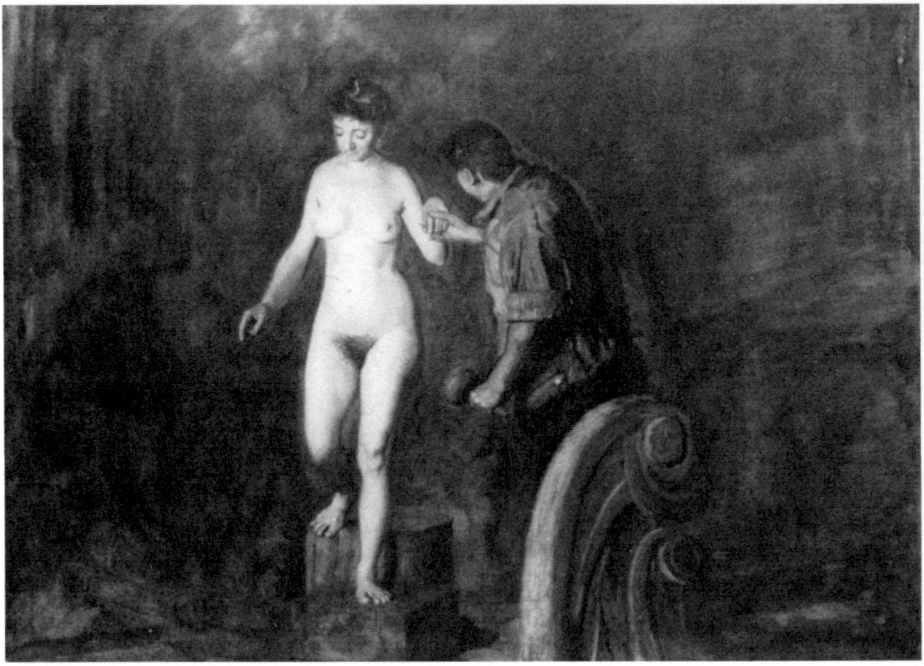

18 Thomas Eakins, *William Rush and His Model*, 1907-8

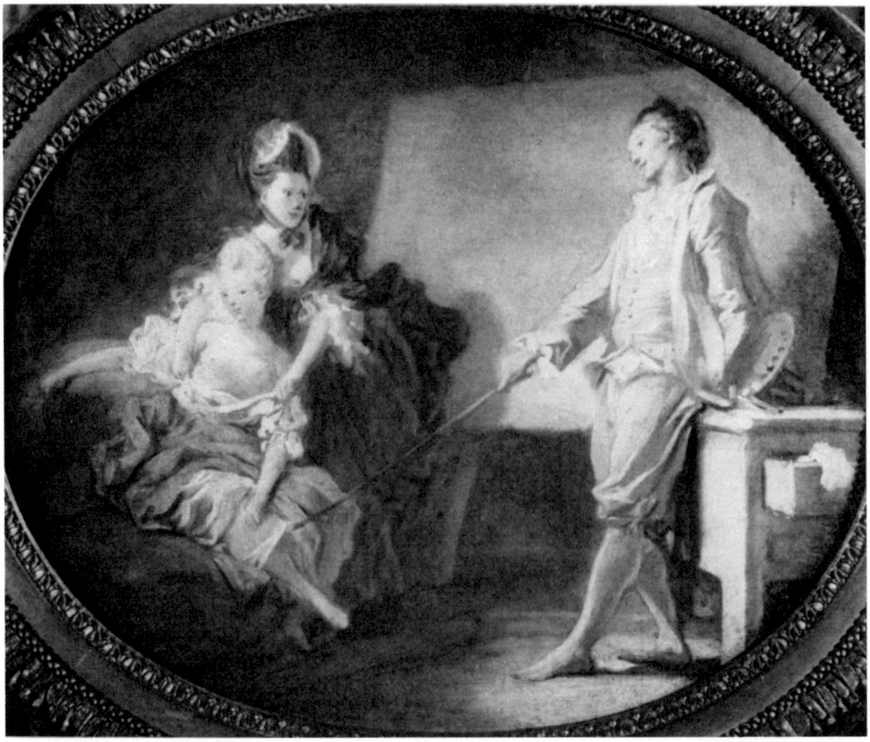

19 Jean Honoré Fragonard, *Le Début du modèle*, 1765-72

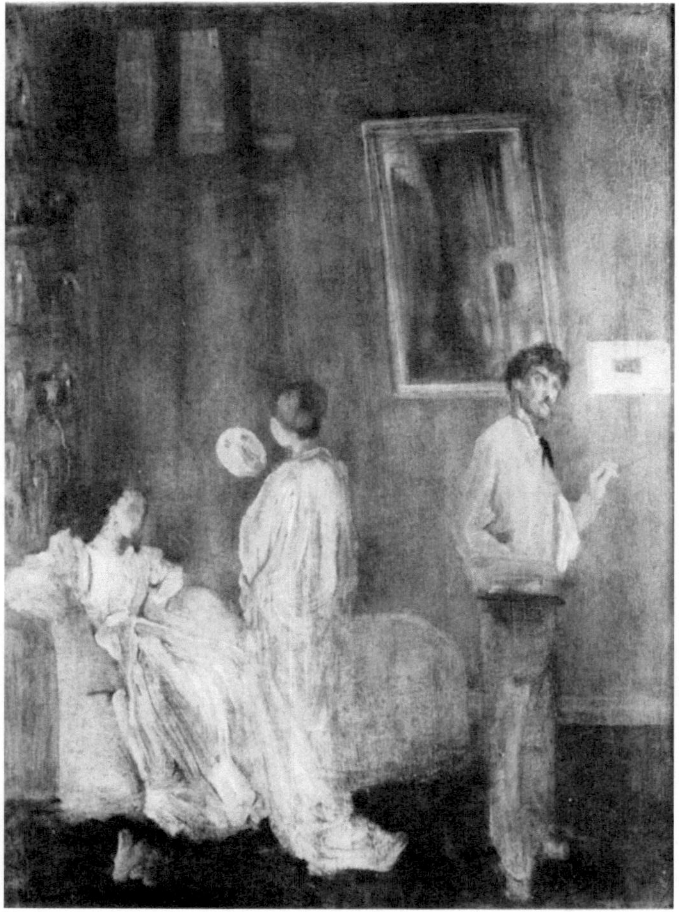

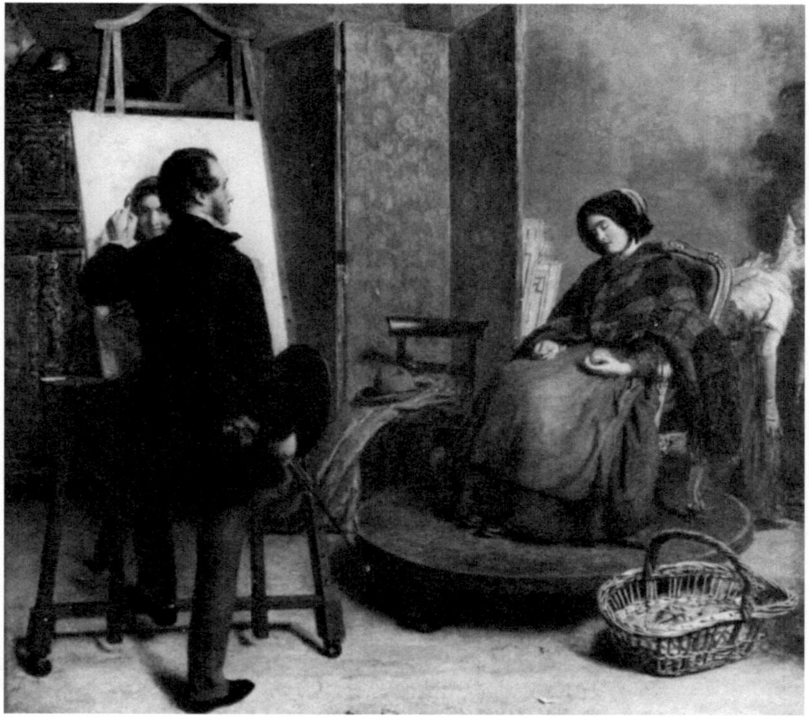

20 (*left*) James Abbott McNeill Whistler, sketch for *Artist in the Studio*

21 (*above*) W.P. Frith, *The Sleeping Model*, 1853

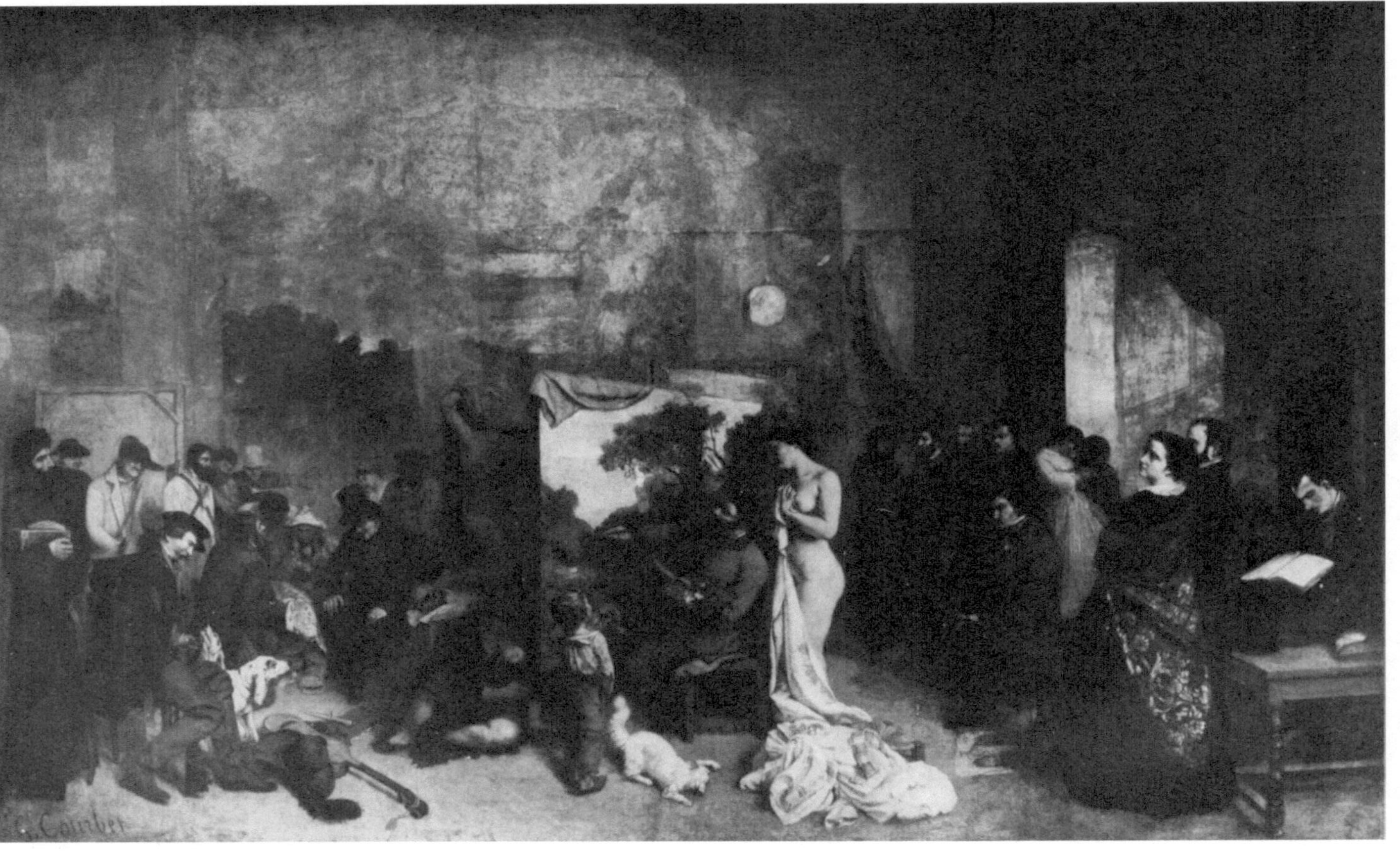

22 Gustave Courbet, *The Painter's Studio*, 1855

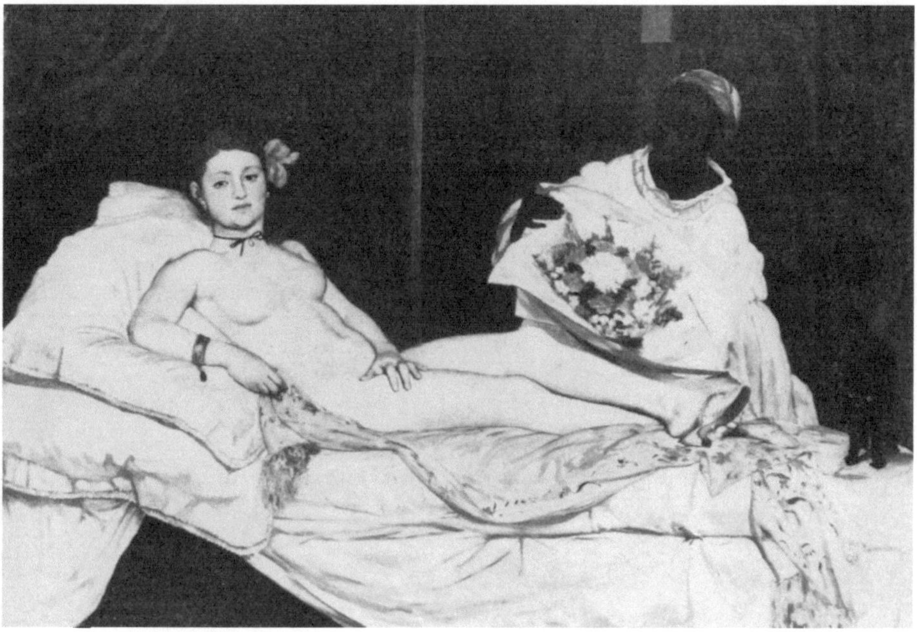

23 Edouard Manet, *Olympia*, 1865

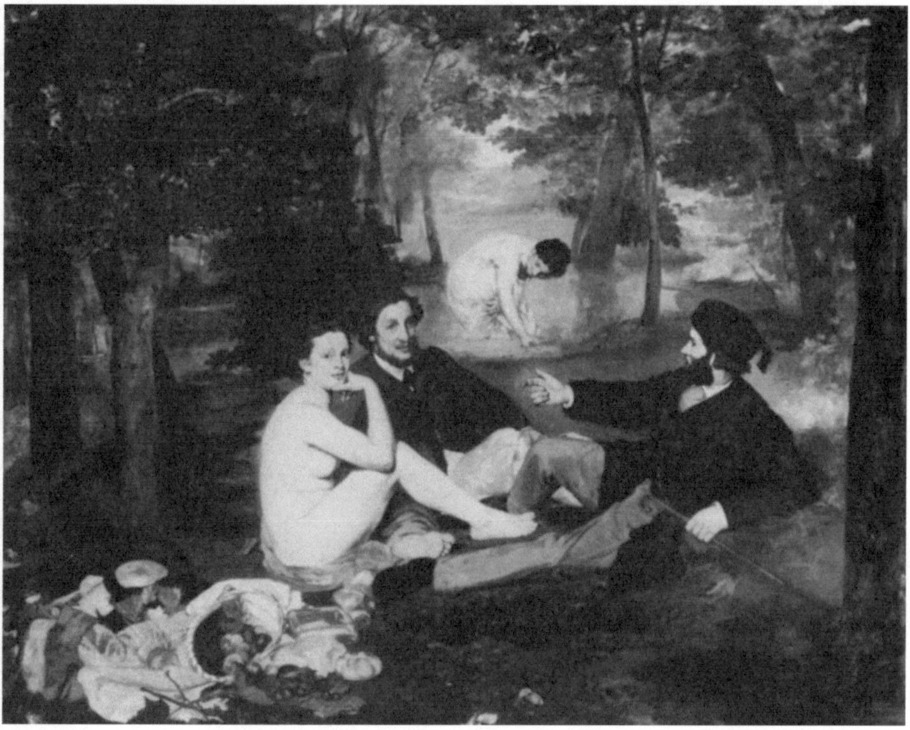

24 Edouard Manet, *Le Déjeuner sur l'herbe*

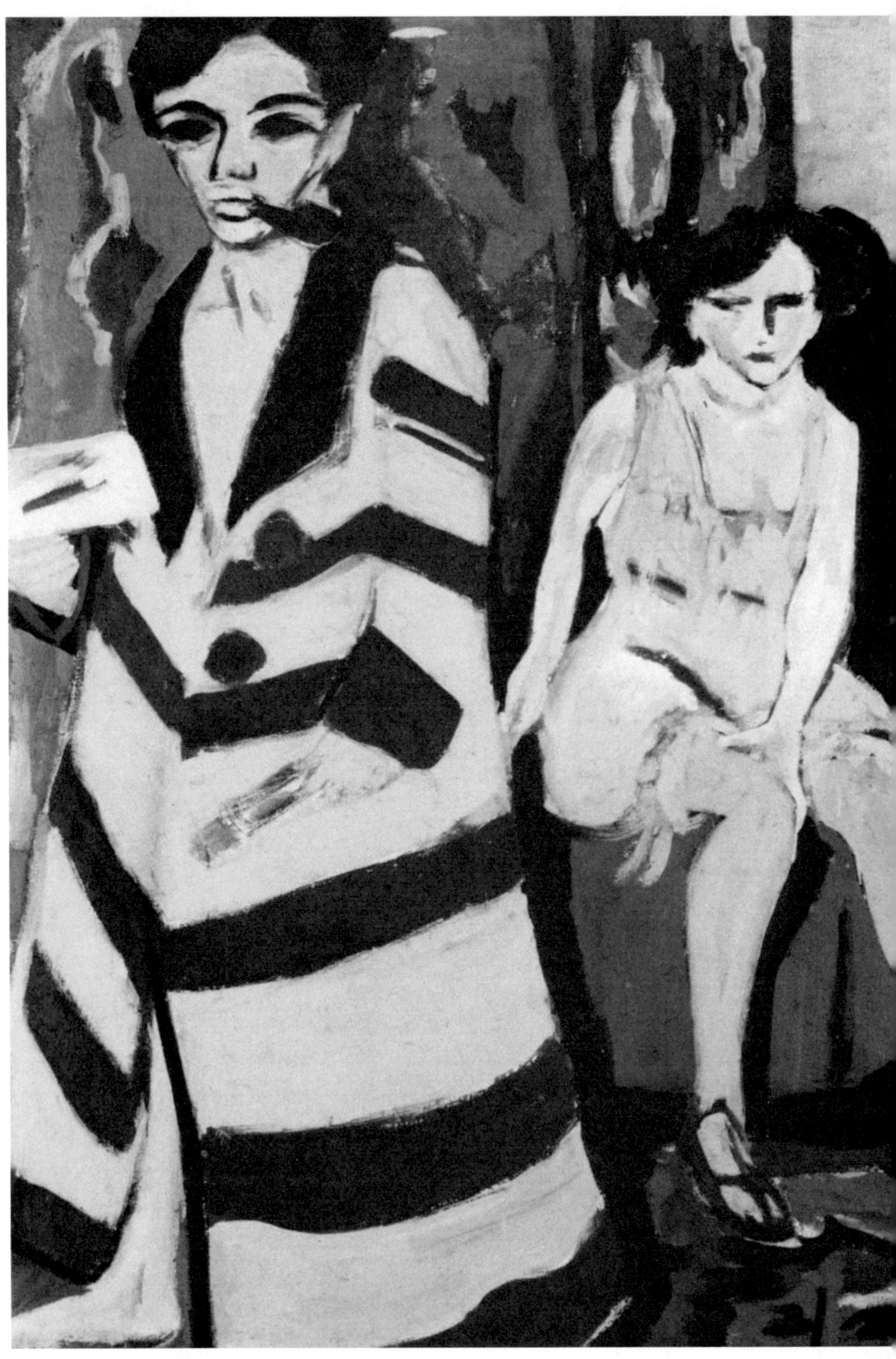

25 Ernst Ludwig Kirchner, *Self-portrait with Model,* 1907

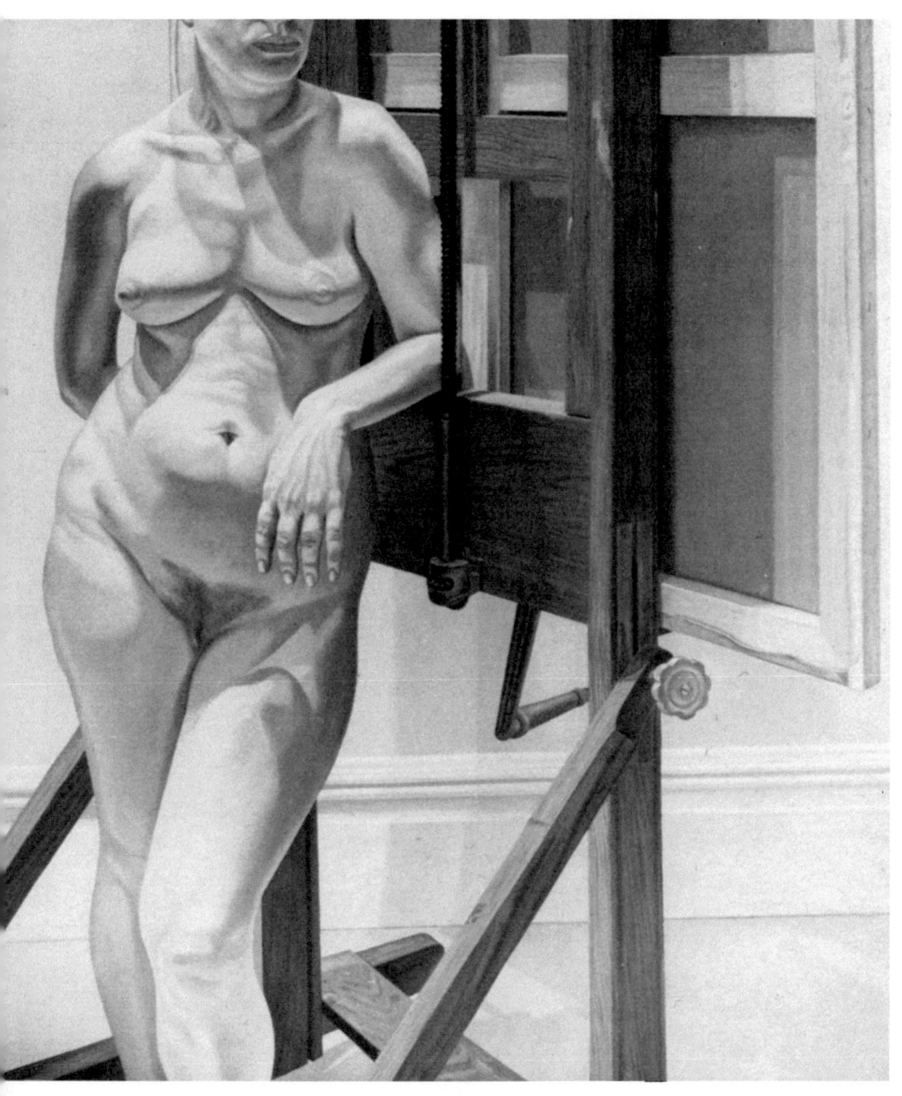

6 Philip Pearlstein, *Model Standing by Easel*, 1974

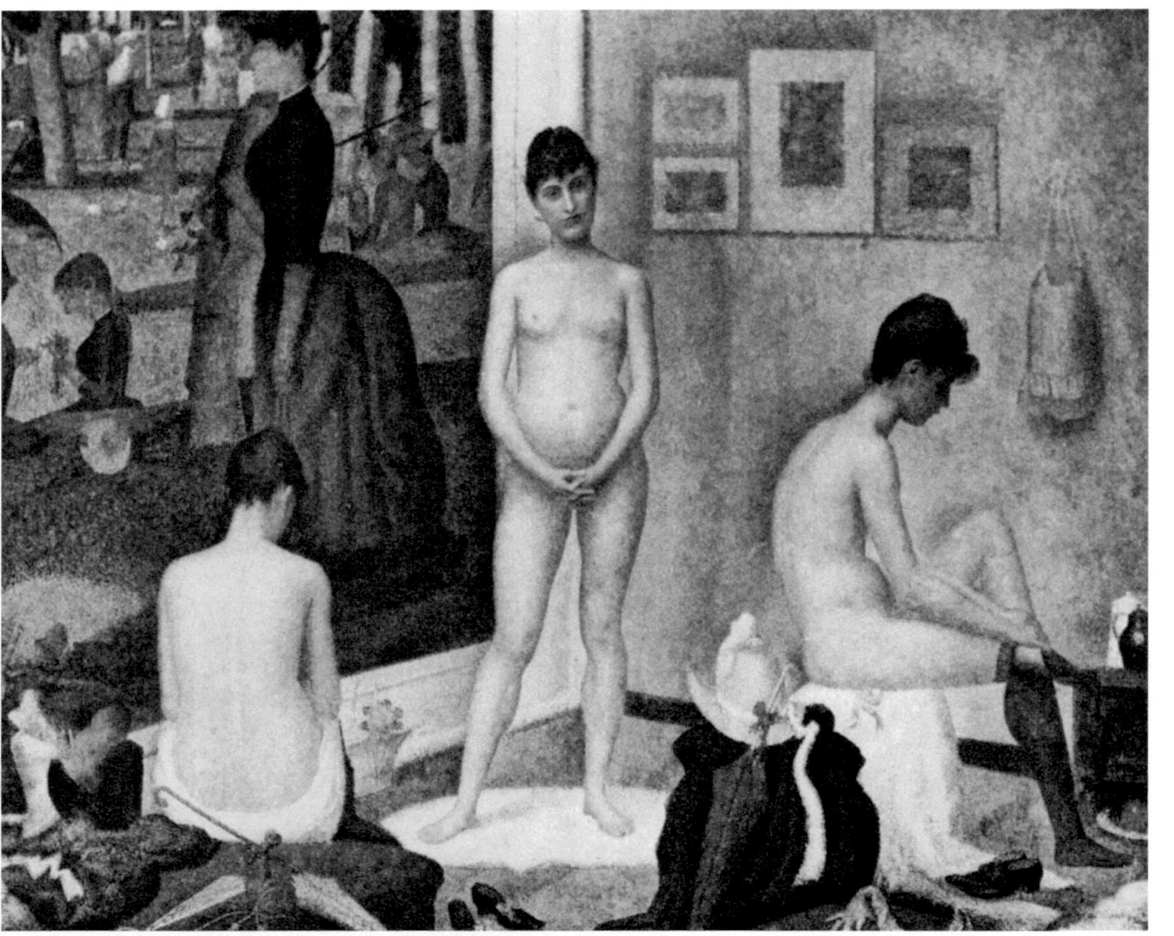

27 Georges Seurat, *Les Poseuses*, 1887-8, photograph © 1982 by The Barnes Foundation, Merion, Pa.

who for a $500 picture pay five thousand — a beautiful portrait of an ugly daughter — you known Duncan — or a fat man to be made with no belly? Do they come here — where is your wife? Behind the curtain — no this will not do!

The hero is only allowed to make his model his bride because she is not a professional model (her mother is horrified to find her posing) but an artist helping the hero out. Bergeret's belief in the unsuitability of marrying one's model is not questioned. As Duncan tells Bergeret, she is a model, yes — 'But not as Paris knows the word.'

The true change brought by Bohemia, the forcing of conventional society to accept the values of the artistic community as different but equal to its own, is not mirrored in this basically old-fashioned play. Before that could happen, *la vie de bohème* had to upgrade its image into a glamorous and exciting way of life that could hold up its head against the larger society surrounding it — in fact, could make that society bow to Bohemia's conventions.

The image of life and love among the artists presented in *Trilby* played a crucial part in promoting the acceptability of Bohemian life and the model who played an important part within it. Harry Furniss wrote in *Some Victorian Women*:

Du Maurier, in writing *Trilby*, aroused the curiosity of the ordinary domesticated woman . . . It was largely due to the studio life depicted so charmingly by Du Maurier, and Trilby sitting for the 'Altogether,' and the fact that it was published in a high-class magazine emanating from a publishing firm, that made the novel such a commercial success. Its dramatization only heightened its interest. After this there was a boom in studio life, and female models in particular. Society women became positively jealous of them.[10]

As a result artists became men, models became women and the art world became exciting and even a little dangerous. Modelling had always been a mecca for poor but pretty females but Bohemia made it a mecca for women of all classes. Mothers like Mrs Pettigrew sent her three young daughters off to the great Millais, music-hall artistes took to modelling for artists as a way to promote themselves, upper-class women turned into artists' groupies and threw in their lot with the painters and sculptors — the not-so-famous as well as the famous, since being an artist was developing a cachet which had nothing to do with success.

This upgrading of the art world into a glamorous Bohemia which led to the male artist-female model relationship becoming socially acceptable, is a development which can be traced through literature's attitude to the model. In 'Little Hunchback', one of Hume's stories of penniless artists (all of whom in a particularly English touch are approaching success by the end of the book), a dancer poses nude out of love for a hunchback sculptor. The sculptor dies and the dancer's broken-hearted appearance in a pantomime on the night of his funeral is a late example of the punitive Victorian ethic which decreed suffering to any woman who took off her clothes outside marriage. In *Trilby* the model heroine is allowed to be in love with an artist and he with her, but she is not allowed to marry him. In fact she has to die for stepping out of her station.

By 1907 the possibility of modelling without punishment appears. Arthur Ransome's chapter on artist's studios in *Bohemian in London* presents the model as the artist's companion, cooking his lunchtime eggs and accompanying him to a party in the evening. By 1914 the model goes home with the artist after the party and the relationship comes out of the closet. The Bohemian art students in Gilbert Cannan's *Mendel* of 1916 make their models their mistresses. After the First World War, Bohemia has become shorthand for life and love among the artists. By the 1920s to pair an artist with a model is enough to suggest the artist's enthusiastic sexuality and to call a woman a model is to suggest her sexual accessibility. The lusty artist John Bidlake in Huxley's *Point Counterpoint* is surrounded by models, and the sexually knowing Minette in Lawrence's *Women in Love* is a model.

Bohemia came into its own in England in the interwar years of this century, when models and artists living a Bohemian existence according to their own rules within the more sober society surrounding them, became a reality. It is the world of Soho cafés, Chelsea parties and Hampstead studios. The female models' status improved and the artist-model relationship could be publicly admitted and openly envied. The predominantly female image the model had gained by the 1920s is a familiar one from interwar fiction and biography, in which she is shown connected to a certain kind of artist whose advanced artistic ideas were supported by an advanced Bohemian lifestyle.

Bohemia collapsed in the fifties, at the same time as New York and its abstract art replaced Paris as the art capital of the West. Bohemia became a youth movement, a fashion, a statement of generation separation involving flat shoes, black stockings and New Orleans jazz. In the sixties no artistic lifestyle could produce anything to compare with the drugs, the music, the communes and the sexual freedom of the hippies, and many artists, as if in recognition of this, began to produce abstract or pop art as if desperate to take their art out of society or to paint society's more ordinary aspects.

Bohemia died, but the myth it gave birth to did not. The idea of notorious artist-model relationships proved so exciting to the public mind that the more mundane face of modelling was forgotten. The male model getting to his 10 a.m. sitting in time to remove his clothes for the sculpture students, got lost in the glare that emanated from the glowing artist and model relationship that was as much about life between the sheets as in the studio.

Bohemia's most extraordinary achievement is to have remade modelling in its own image. Today we see the models of the past through a Bohemian veil, ignorant of the fact that males modelled as well as females, children modelled, that women modelled who went home to their own beds when the work was finished.

The Bohemian image survives today. It does so because there is no satisfactory contemporary picture of modelling with which to replace it. It has left us with an out-dated image of the lusty male artist and his delectable female model, an image which was developed in mid-nineteenth-century France and exported to England. It is telling the way models are always talked of in terms of the past, as in the Rossetti and Augustus John queries with which this book began. The reason is that few facts about modelling today

have come to fill the gap Bohemia has left. And those that
have are too dull to interest anyone.

Notes

1 William M. Thackeray, *The Adventures of Philip* (3 vols., London,
1862), vol. 1, ch. 10.
2 *Punch*, 8 September 1883.
3 William M. Thackeray, *Vanity Fair*, 1847, (Pan, 1980), ch. LXIV,
p. 685.
4 Lester Lurgan, *Bohemian Blood* (London, 1910), ch. 7.
5 Henry Stacey Marks, *Pen and Pencil Sketches* (2 vols., London,
1894), vol. 1, p. 32.
6 Joseph Hatton, *Queen of Bohemia* (2 vols., London, 1877), vol. 1,
ch. 3.
7 Henry James, *The Europeans* (London, 1878), ch. 12.
8 Fergus Hume, *When I Lived in Bohemia* (Bristol, 1892), p. 4.
9 *The Bohemian*, 8 January 1887.
10 Harry Furniss, *Some Victorian Women* (London, 1923), pp. 101-2.

6
The Stereotype

The stereotype of models — how the public perceives them — has fluctuated over the past two centuries. An impression of these changes can be got from the jokes in *Punch*, which for nearly a century and a half have offered a commentary on how models have looked from the vantage point of the middle and upper classes. Taken together, these jokes present a bird's-eye view of the changing stereotype of the artist's model from 1840 to the present day.

Both the models' history and the models' status are reflected in the cartoons. The account is not complete since *Punch* came too late for the eighteenth-century preoccupation with casts and was too respectable to comment on the nineteenth-century worry over the link between modelling and sex. But despite the gaps, *Punch*'s picture of modelling, simplified and satirized though it is, supports the facts that have emerged. In the nineteenth century, *Punch* noted the professional status of the Victorian models as well as the artists' superior attitude towards them. In the twentieth century, *Punch* chronicled the growing use of the female model, the decline in the importance of modelling after the Second World War and its fate today as the preserve of the amateur.

For the first twenty years of publication there were no jokes showing models as professionals. Instead jokes about modelling were based on the artist persuading friends and family to pose. Typical is the Enthusiastic Artist of 15 June 1861, who tells his friend to 'keep that expression for one moment. You've got such a splendid head for my picture of the Canting Hypocrite.' The introduction of the professional model as a cartoon character did not take place until after 1860 when it coincided with an increase in the number and size of the cartoons the journal carried. From then until the First World War, there were several artists' model jokes each year. An early example of the professional model joke appeared on 12 September 1863:

Model   Fine day, sir.
Painter   (aghast) Fine — good heavens man, where's your beard?
Model   Just made my whiskers a wee thing decent with the shears.
Painter   Then you're an utterly ruined man, sir and I'm very sorry for you. You're not worth 2d. Good morning.

The image of the model in this cartoon — male, lower class, comic and too stupid to act in his own best interest — was to hold good until the end of the First World War and appeared periodically after it. Although not all artists could have been upper class and polite and not all models lower class and sent by heaven to try the artist, the characterization of the model as someone to be borne with good grace was widespread at this period. The tone of the joke below, in which the artist 'gloomily continues painting' when the Comic Model turns out to have lost a leg in an unromantic manner, echoes that of the nineteenth-century artists when discussing models in their autobiographies (fig. 16):

R.A. (who has engaged Chelsea Pensioner as model looking forward with interest to stirring narrative of battlefield where he was disabled)   And where did you lose your leg?
Veteran   Round the corner, sir, at Mrs. Wembley's. You see, when I left off soldiering, I went into the furniture business as carman. Unloading van, pianner fell on my leg and broke it. Then I got into the orspital. *(R.A. gloomily continues painting.)*[1]

Punch chronicled other aspects of the model that have been noted, like the male model as jack-of-all-trades. In 1869 the model is shown in charge of hats at an art school *conversazione* and of course he loses them. In 1870 models are shown vying to take the artist's pictures to the Academy:

100

Artist to model who has called to ask if he shall take his pictures down to the R.A. You're too late Smithers. Bulford was here just now and I promised him the job.
Smithers Very sorry sir. But — if so be — Sir, it might 'appen sir — in case they was — to be fetched away.
Artist If they're rejected you mean — I'll let you know.

Punch also recorded child models. On 14 December 1895, 'Little Guttersnipe (who is getting quite used to posing)' asks the artist 'Will yer want me ter tike my bun down?' Child models clearly posed problems for the painters who had to deal with them. According to McLaren, when a pretty girl Whistler had glimpsed in the street was brought to his studio he saw to his horror that her red hair was 'frizzed and curled in a way that he considered frightful'.[2] Few female models were illustrated until about 1880, but their numbers increased with the age of the century. Character models, that is models with strongly defined characteristics such as age, eccentricity or unconventional looks, were rarely female. Female models from the 1880s onwards were distinguished by their youth and beauty and shared with their male counterparts a working class-background and an absence of brains. On 16 April 1902, a painter asks his pretty model if she has shown herself to a fellow artist:

Well, I've been to see him; but directly I got into his studio, 'Why,' he said, 'You've got a head like a Botticelli.' I don't know what a Botticelli is, but I didn't go there to be called names, so I come away!

The claims to equality that accompanied the models' view of themselves as professionals, were seen to be as ridiculous when women made them as when men did. In 1900 a cheeky lady model adopts the artist's mode of address (fig. 14):

Painter You can stand down and rest, Model
Model Aw right, Hartist[3]

Her appealing insouciance leaves a pleasanter taste than that left by the jokes about male models who see themselves on the same level as the artists, but the awful vision revealed by the crumbling of barriers between the classes remains the same. There is no doubt such jokes were based on experience — the artist's experience, that is. It must have been aggravating to employ models who refused not only to know their own place but put down yours as well. Black-and-white artist Harry Furniss employed a model who was horrified when she discovered she was to be used for a *Punch* drawing.

> 'For *Punch* is it? Well, I do hope you won't mention that I sat for it — you see, I only sit to fashionable portrait painters for hands, and if it were known I sat to a comic artist I should lose my prestige.' As a matter of fact, the model was, like so many of them are, very anxious to impress the artist engaging them with their own value and importance. She was talking rot and I told her so.[4]

As far as female models were concerned, this patronizing attitude died out after the First World War, though it took longer with the men. Awareness of the model's change in status can be seen in 1926 when *Punch* took the model as a subject for its 'Manners and Modes' series (fig. 15):

> *In the Nineties: The Artist* It's one o'clock, Miss Tomkins. We'll stop now, and I'll send you in a cup of cocoa to drink with your sandwiches.
> *Today: The Model* Quarter to one, old thing. What about ringing up a taxi? I'm due to lunch at the Fitz at one.[5]

On 21 May 1924, a guest at a grand party asks (fig. 17):

> 'Who is that rather wonderful person Lady Tremayne is welcoming so effusively?'
> 'Oh, that's Pepita — Johnstein's model, you know.'
> 'Gracious! Lady Tremayne *is* getting on in the world.'

The joke is a comment on the interwar phenomenon in which artists became outrageous personalities and their models shared in their glory. Johnstein was an amalgam of the painter Augustus John and the sculptor Jacob Epstein, *Punch*'s symbols at this time for the bohemian and ultra-modern artist.

Male models between the wars were frequently shown modelling for illustrators, plausibly so, since illustration remained the life-based art which painting and sculpture were ceasing to be. They were fitted into the comic model format established in the nineteenth century; in fact some of the jokes read as if their creators had been leafing through the previous century's copies of *Punch* for inspiration: 'You look like an old Titian', says the artist to his model. 'Well, you aren't much to write home about yourself' he replies.[6] A chatty cockney model commits the nineteenth-century error of regarding himself on a level with the artist — only the year is 1930: 'It must be three years ago, Sir, since we last had the pleasure of co-operating.'[7]

The 1950s saw another change in the cartoonists' presentation of the artist's model: always female, she became classless and she removed her clothes. *Punch*'s first nude model joke appeared in 1938 but it was not until the 1950s that she took over as the stereotype of the artist's model. In 1956, a teacher coaxes a reluctant model out to his class: 'All right Miss Frobisher, on our honour we promise not to laugh.'[8] Anton illustrates the female model who just happens to be naked as she rocks the baby in the pram as she poses or has her hair permed while the sculptor copies her torso.[9] A surreal quality marks these jokes in which both the artist and his model inhabit another world with its own set of laws and logic. 'For heaven's sake Mr. Morgan, I only came up to complain about the banging', says the nude woman as she poses for a sculptor in 1966.[10]

At the end of the 1960s two more changes occurred. Model jokes became rarer. And they lost the topicality that had distinguished them right through the 1950s when they repeatedly pointed up the madness of having a model pose for abstract art. By the sixties and seventies, the model as the subject of satire and social observation had died. Models were either imagined in terms of the past or were seen as the nude attractions for the pop-eyed visitor to the studio.

Its role of purveyor of humour to the higher classes affected what *Punch* said about models and its great silence, as might be expected, was on the link between models and sexuality. *Punch* was not unaware of the prostitute-model link. The first issue of the magazine hinted that lady models often doubled as ladies of the evening. However that was the first and last time this aspect of female modelling was to be noted in this respectable magazine.[11]

Punch's respectability ensured that the strongest reference to the female model's sexuality in the nineteenth century was to their good looks, and even this slight suggestion tended to be undercut by the comic stereotype until the First World War. For years *Punch* was so successful at divorcing art from nudity that a cartoon in 1922 in which a young woman with her eyes on a nude statue says to her friend, 'That reminds me, Helen. We must buy some undies, to-day' stands out as positively indecent.[12]

Although *Punch*'s respectability ensured that there was both coyness and a time-lag in the presentation of nudity compared to its treatment in more raffish magazines like *Men Only*, it did finally get round to recording this aspect of modelling. As the sexual climate warmed up after the First World War, and as Bohemia began to improve the social acceptability of the artist-model relationship, jokes referring to nudity began to appear. In 1921 a painter is asked 'Ever painted in the nude?' 'No', he replies, 'My wardrobe never gets as low as all that.'[13] From 1924, when a thinly draped and pretty model poses for a sculptor working on a nude statue, wispy draperies become *Punch*'s way of signalling that nude modelling is in progress. In 1938 *Punch* showed a nude model. 'Take care Mr. Todhunter, I've a bad bruise just there',[14] she says, as the sculptor starts to copy her leg. Nude joke No. 2 follows in 1939, this time showing a male model who stands with no clothes on having his hand copied for an exit sign.[15] But it was not till the 1950s that the lady nude took over as the model stereotype.

Punch may have shied away from the model-sex link but it was vocal on the subject of Bohemia. It faithfully recorded the arrival of the new Bohemian ideas into England, showing the major change in the Bohemian image from Bohemianism as companionship between men to Bohemianism which needed women, in particular female models, to achieve its status. The Bohemian who makes an occasional appearance at the turn of the century is a sort of comic minor criminal. 'La vie de bohème' is the title of a joke by Phil May on 3 September 1902:

> *First Bohemian (to second ditto)*   I can't for the life of me think why you wasted all that time haggling with that tailor chap, and beating him down, when you know, old chap, you won't be able to pay him at all.
> *Second Bohemian*   Ah, that's *it*. *I* have a conscience. I want the poor chap to lose as little as possible!

The twentieth-century Bohemian puts in much more frequent appearances. In fact from 1923 to the outbreak of the Second World War, the Bohemian artist with untidy hair, scruffy clothes, wide-brimmed black hat and outlandishly dressed lady companion was one of *Punch*'s three main artist targets along with The Genius and The Modern Artist. In 1921 a full-page cartoon entitled 'The Romance of Bohemia' shows several respectable couples in a Soho restaurant spending 'a most thrilling hour imagining each other to be celebrated Bohemians with scandalous pasts'.[16]

Punch in the nineteenth century aligned itself with the artists' view of themselves as professionals and pillars of society. In 1882, artists share the same manners and standards as their patrons. In a cartoon entitled 'Lights and Shadows of Portrait Painting — The Finishing Touch', the artist's studio is as opulent as a drawing room, as it would have to have been to make it a suitable place for the upper classes to visit to have their portraits painted. Feelings of disdain for his patrons are never to be shown as the painter conforms to their standards:

> *Fair Sitter's Mama*   I'm *sure* the nose is not aquiline enough, Mr. Sopely!
> *The Artist (with one dextrous sweep of his brush)* Is that better?
> *Fair Sitter's Mama*   Oh, ever so much! Now the likeness is simply *perfect*.
> *Fair Sitter's Papa (who is always so contradictory)* Hum! Now *I* consider that last touch has spoilt the likeness altogether! (Sopely's brush was perfectly dry — and so was

his canvas!)[17]

By the 1920s the artist-patron relationship had under-
gone a great change. The painter saw no reason to spruce-up
his lifestyle for any patron, and the patron understood that
he had to accept the artist's unconventional way of life and
view of art. In 1926, the Sitter says to the Portrait Painter,
'But my dear sir, I haven't got a beard.' The artist replies,
'But I have, and I always subordinate my sitters' individuality
to my own.'[18]

Punch illustrated the change from artist as member of the
establishment to artist as crazy outsider through the figure
of the Bohemian artist. In contrast to the impeccable social
behaviour that had been the nineteenth-century artist's key
to social acceptance, the Bohemian conventions of the
twentieth century demanded a lifestyle of free love, alcohol,
unconventionality and intensity.

The beards and black hats which signify the artist as outsider in *Punch* supply a contrast with the conservative dress
of the previous century's artists. There were lots of jokes
about the Bohemian artists' appearance in the interwar years.
A couple in 1926 eye a modern sculpture and the Nervous
Little Man says to the Lady, 'I say old thing, I wouldn't
laugh quite so loud. Half the room looks as if it might have
done it.'[19]

Punch recorded a seesaw exchange in the reputations of
artists and models over the two centuries. While in the
nineteenth century the artist was presented seriously and
the model was the butt of the joke, in the twentieth century
it was the artist who was found to be funny and the model
who is taken relatively seriously. It is through the replacement of models as comic targets with mad art and madder
artists that the cartoons reveal the model's improved status
between the wars.

In the nineteenth century, as a result of its alignment with
the artists' point of view, *Punch* was unable to conceive of
models as anything but frustrating or amusing for the artist.
In the twentieth century *Punch* decided that artists were
irresistible comic targets, which meant that models were
moved out of the line of fire. A joke of 1933 entitled 'In-
difference' shows the back of a wispily draped model and an

artist painting a modernistic, that is, unintelligible, front view.[20] Like many jokes of the period, its humour comes from the fact that the artist is bothering to use a model at all, given the unlikeness to life of the abstract end product. It is the artist who is ridiculous, not the model.

Punch tried to link the interwar model's glamour and improved social status to the new female types which so excited the age, the mannequin and the film star. The film star is noted in the cartoons for her power, her money and her marriages. The mannequin is noted for the perversity that leads the daughters of the upper classes to scrabble for jobs as mannequins in Harridge's undie parade, as *Punch* has Lady Magnolia doing in 1933.[21] (*Punch* was fascinated by the mannequin phenomenon. In 1928, a daughter tells her aristocratic mother she has a job. 'Not a mannequin', her mother asks in awe. 'Oh no darling', replies her daughter, 'But I'm going to help dress one.'[22] The model is noted for the extraordinary upward mobility that has landed her in society's drawing rooms.

But fascinating though it is to see *Punch* trying to fit the artist's model into the brand new category of independent wage-earning women who make a career from their looks, the fact that there are fewer model than film star and mannequin jokes suggests that the journal understood that the model was less important than the other two. Compared to the film and clothing industries, the sums involved in art were on a cottage-industry level. The model may have mattered to individual artists, but the looks and talents of the mannequins and film stars were responsible for selling commodities worth millions. The small number of cartoons dealing with the newly grand lady model show she was only a fringe element socially, and an unimportant one financially in the scene *Punch* saw as its duty to comment upon.

With the passing of the notorious Bohemian artist went the notorious artist's model. The new aesthetic of abstraction did not need models so much as it needed female companions to cook the food and clean the clothes, and love in a garret with an unsuccessful artist, the sixties version of *la vie de bohème*, is presented as duller than a more conventional existence. Says the worn-out artist's lady in 1967, 'Sometimes I feel I'd like to live a normal life — marriage divorce, alimony . . .'[23] Bohemianism has become outmoded and its values have lost their power to shock.

The social misbehaviour which marked Bohemianism faded before the sexual revolution of the sixties and seventies when the cartoonists' targets became call girls, secretaries in bed with their bosses, and middle-aged women eyeing ads for mens' underpants on the escalators. What could possibly be bold about Bohemianism in the age of *Last Tango in Paris*? As one man in a *Punch* film queue says to another: 'I must say I'm enjoying my metamorphosis from dirty old man to avant-garde eroticist.'[24]

In the last two decades, *Punch* has charted the decline of the model's importance. On 13 September 1967, the magazine ran a page of cartoons by ffoukes entitled 'Artists and Models'. All the artists were dead, or if alive so old they qualified as old masters, and all the models were nude and female. One joke showed Cranach with a Venus on his easel saying to his overweight model, 'If you're going to go on working for me you'll have to lay off the apfel strudel.' In another a prostitute tells her client as Toulouse-Lautrec sits sketching at the end of their bed, 'You mustn't mind Henri — he draws very quickly.' On 1 November 1967, Heath did a similar page called 'Model of the Year', a comic tale of a photographer who rebels against the fad for skinny fashion models and launches a fat model on the world of fashion.

What is so fascinating about these two pages is that while Heath's photographic model story is topical and satirizes a contemporary development in the fashion world, ffoukes's artists' models page is not. In 1967 there *were* no developments in the world of artist and model to satirize in a way that would have made sense to the readers of *Punch*. Artists' models had no image beyond an outdated one. Models were either the classy fashion kind paid to make clothes look wearable and desirable — the young women who had developed from their satirized origins as aristocratic mannequins to become the aristocrats of the modelling world — or they were the photographic models who posed in the nude for girly magazines. *Punch* picked up this development in 1967, with a photographer telling his nude model as she poses with a cricket bat, 'For heaven's sake, Lucille, hold the damned thing properly. This is for a man's magazine.'

Artists's models are rare in the sixties and seventies but when they do appear they are funny in ways that have little to do with the contemporary art scene. In 1975, Honeysett shows a cluster of clothed, middle-aged women posing on the model's throne, while the similarly aged and dressed flower-arranging class uses them as models for their flower arrangements.[25] A cartoon in 1974 displaying Bill Tidy's taste for the oversized passions of working-class folks, illustrates Mrs Hinchcliffe's fury when she discovers the 'nudes' class ringed in the further education catalogue and storms off to the school to discover her husband is the model.[26] A cartoon in 'Artists in Clink', Larry's comment on prison paintings, shows a lady visitor reclining nude over two chairs as the prisoner draws her from behind his bars.[27]

Topical comments are reserved for art, whose successive phases over the last two decades have been satirized with gusto. 'More and more local authorities are taking on artists and sculptors' reads the text on Quentin Blake's 'Support your local artist' page. One cartoon shows a fat, bald councillor asking a thin hairy arty type 'And this Francis Bacon, if we can get him — would he be right for the Sunnyside Old Folks Leisure Lounge?'[28] Metal sculptures, white on white paintings ('Excuse me, is this gallery just empty, or is this an exhibition?'), pop, op, dealers' language ('These belong to his cautious, rather groping, formative period') are all satirized, whereas the best that can be done with models is to have an artist say to his naked model, who has asked him for a light, 'Don't you ever carry matches?'[29] It may be amusing, but it is hardly topical.

The inability of the cartoonists to make topical jokes about artists' models reflects their irrelevance to present-day society. So little is known about modelling in this era of the amateur part-timer that it cannot be satirized. Nowadays model jokes fall into two categories, both based on the model as nude female. One puts her in situations of innocent nudity, of the visitor to the studio bumping into the furniture because he cannot take his eyes off her. The other uses her to make jokes about the artists of the past. Neither is topical, but because there is nothing to replace them with they refuse to die.

Notes

1 'Quite Another Story', *Punch* 27 April 1904.
2 A. McLaren Young, M. Macdonald and R. Spencer, *The Paintings of James McNeill Whistler* (2 vols., Yale University Press, 1980), Text Vol., p. 203.
3 *Punch*, 10 October 1900.
4 Harry Furniss, *Some Victorian Women* (London, 1923), pp. 104-5.
5 *Punch*, Almanack for 1927, 1 November 1926.
6 Ibid., 12 December 1928.
7 Ibid., 3 September 1930.
8 Ibid., 5 December 1956.
9 Ibid., 29 September 1954; 30 March 1955.
10 Ibid., 17 August 1966.
11 Ibid., vol. 1, p. 33.
12 Ibid., 13 December 1922.
13 Ibid., 4 May 1921.
14 Ibid., 1 June 1938.
15 Ibid., 8 February 1939.
16 Ibid., 23 March 1921.
17 Ibid., 15 July 1882.
18 Ibid., 11 August 1926.
19 Ibid., 21 July 1926.
20 Ibid., 29 March 1933.
21 Ibid., 5 April 1933.
22 Ibid., 16 May 1928.
23 Ibid., 1 March 1967.
24 Ibid., 21 March 1973.
25 Ibid., 21 May 1975.
26 Ibid., 11 December 1974.
27 Ibid., 28 March 1973.
28 Ibid., 27 March 1974.
29 Ibid., 20 March 1974; ibid., 23 October 1968; ibid., 31 May 1967.

7
High and Low Writing

Even allowing for the odd affair between artist and model, or the cases of artists' obsessions with the looks of particular women, there is a huge gap between the fantasy of the mistress-model and the fact that models come in two sexes, all ages and a variety of shapes and sizes.

This gap has been encouraged by the literature on the subject. The literature of art consists of high and low writing. High writing is scholarly. Low writing is anecdotal. High writing cannot get its mouth round the word model while low writing relishes its utterance, often with a leer on its lips and a glint in its eye. It is hard to say which has done models most damage — the scholars' silence or the anecdotes in which models as mistresses and models as inspiration have been enthusiastically discussed but the factual aspects of their lives ignored.

Low writing about art — tales of the artists' models is the form it most commonly takes — has constantly distorted the facts about modelling. This century has seen the publication of several of these anecdotal books. *The Courtezan Olympia: An Intimate Survey of Artists and Their Mistress-Models* written by C.J. Bulliet and published in 1930 is typical of the genre in its lip-licking belief that 'nudity worth while, be it in painting or in sculpture, has a pelvic impulse in the artist as well as a cranial' and in its double-meanings: 'The model must be felt as feminine before she can be laid on canvas.'[1] The way that model is synonymous with female is a basic part of the distortion of such books, which must be seen as contributing to the mythology that has wrapped itself like a divine cloud round models rather than attempts to supply facts about them.

Facts are not the strong point of any of these books. 'I shall relate the story of Raphael and La Fornarina as I have woven it together from threads and indications in various sources, historical or fictitious. I do not, however, for one moment pretend that the story as I am narrating it is historically correct',[2] explains Rappoport in *Famous Artists and Their Models*, an apology which could be echoed by most books of this sort. Although based on creditable sources, the meagre information they contain is generously buttered with fantasy and then presented in the anecdotal terms which are a convention of the genre. Bulliet, master of the double-meaning, decorates the basic Greek original when he retells the story of Phryne:

> We prefer to imagine him, not at his leisure, but breathless and excited — his topaz mistress revealing herself nude in the full light for him, and for him alone, and the two conspiring to do a daring thing — to promulgate a naked lady in marble. Not quite naked, Phryne teased him — she'd hide her chief charm with her little hand, like this. 'Hold it!' shouted Praxiteles.[3]

High writing on the other hand pretends models do not exist. Entries under model in library catalogues are either non-existent or sparse in the extreme. Books which document the development of artistic institutions and artistic theory like Nikolaus Pevsner's *Academies of Art Past and Present* and Anthony Blunt's *Artistic Theory in Italy*[4] carry no more than the occasional reference to models. There are no Mayhew-style accounts of modelling in earlier ages. Model autobiographies are thin on the ground. I have found only one and that was French — a thin, ghost-written volume of a nineteenth-century male model called Dubosc who is mentioned in the Goncourts' *Manette Salomon* as possessing the suppleness of youth at 55 years of age.[5] Occasionally autobiographies mention periods in their authors' lives when they did a little modelling: Quentin Crisp in this century and W.G. Robertson in the last are examples of this, both authors, interestingly, men. Outside the autobiographies of Victorian artists where the word 'model' leads inevitably to a chapter of comic accounts of lower-class male models, the word is rare in indices of books about artists. The 1980 *catalogue raisonnée* of Whistler's work is an exception; more common is the indexing of models under their names, which is not the blow for recognition it might seem, since the only reader to recognize them as models is the one who already knows the name.

The split between risqué anecdote and tight-lipped scholarship reflected in the high and low writings about models is a product of the Italian Renaissance. Before the Renaissance the division was not so clearly marked. After it, the gap between the two ways of writing was unbridgeable.

The writers of classical Greece and Rome jumble together artistic theory, art history, feats of the painters and tales of the models as if they are writing a 'Fancy That!' column for a tabloid newspaper. Accounts of statues so beautiful they inspire lust in the spectator, a history of art, and information on artistic practices and standards are all mixed up together. Passages which mention models are of two kinds. Either they name specific models and take the form of anecdotes, usually, since the models named are always women, with titillating overtones. Or they discuss artistic practices, in which case the models are only mentioned indirectly as aids to achieving the required effect.

This classical hodge-podge of information and entertaining stories changed with the advent of the fifteenth-century Italian theorists who in their determination to make a liberal art of the craft of painting threw out the gossip but kept the theory. Writes Alberti firmly in *On Painting* in 1435:

> But we are not interested in knowing who was the inventor of the art of the first painter, since we are not telling stories like Pliny. We are, however, building anew an art of painting about which nothing, as I see it, has been written in this age.[6]

What the Renaissance theorists wished to do was replace the existing workshop-based notion of art with a scientific approach to the subject. They drew courage for this undertaking from their belief that a formula of some kind underlay the perfection of the classical sculptures which were coming to light at this period. Like the Greek and Roman writers, the Renaissance theorists held to the notion of the greatest artists being the ones who could produce a picture that looked like life while it corrected life's flaws. Where they differed was in their devotion to producing theories and giving practical advice on achieving this state.

This newly serious approach to art theory, which saw its role as passing out instruction on how to draw, compose, learn the anatomy of the human body, master perspective and assess subject matter on a scale of frivolous to important, was expressed in a newly serious style. Anecdotes are not entirely dropped, not even by Alberti, but they are brought in to illustrate certain points about the art of painting and not for the love of a good story alone, which is what seems to have motivated the classical writers.

The concentration on drawing, anatomy, proportion, perspective and composition in the interests of better painting is accompanied by a curious silence on the subject of models. The Renaissance theorists' refusal to let the word model flow from the nibs of their pens is particularly frustrating in the light of their belief in accurate drawing from life as a basis of artistic prowess. Though Alberti clearly believes in working from life ('He who dares take everything he fashions from nature will make his hand so skilled that whatever he does will always appear to be drawn from nature'),[7] oblique references to nature replace outright references to models. The furthest he goes is to recommend the faces of well-known and worthy men (including his own, he suggests, if painters feel he has been useful) in history paintings with serious themes, because

> that well-known face will draw to itself first of all the eyes of one who looks at the *istoria*. So great is the force of anything drawn from nature. For this reason, always take from nature that which you wish to paint and always choose the most beautiful.[8]

A similar silence reigns over the writings of Leonardo da Vinci. A recommendation that a painter note gestures stemming from particular emotions supplies a rare reference to modelling:

Note them at once and fix them in your mind, and do not wait until the action of weeping has to be copied from one who poses as if weeping, but without great cause for grief, and then draw it, because such an action, having no real cause, will be neither lifelike nor natural. But it is very good to have noted it first as it occurs, naturally, and then pose somebody in that act, in order to see any necessary detail and draw it.[9]

The notion of a painter setting a model and a model holding a pose is present, but further information on those 'somebodies' who can be posed in not forthcoming.

The Renaissance theorists established the dismissive way scholars would write about the model until the present day. Except for one major hiccup in the form of Vasari, they established the literary divide between high and low writing about models.

Vasari's *Lives of the Artists*, first published in Italy in 1556, is written in a chatty style which unites theory and anecdote in an updated version of the classical writers. Both high and low writing are contained in Vasari. True to the formula, when it is theory that is under discussion, for example, the necessity of learning to draw from life, then models are mentioned in abstract terms as aids to artistic skill. But when theory is left for biography, models are presented as personalities.

In selecting his model anecdotes, Vasari follows the pattern of the classical writers. Vasari's criteria for a model story are that it be scandalous, or amusing, have some connection with the artist under discussion, or involve a famous name. Like his classical predecessors, he is interested in noted beauties, like Ginevra de 'Benci who appeared in a *Visitation* by Ghirlandajo; or in the well-born who mis-behave, like Lucrezia who ran off with Fra Filippo Lippi when in the care of the nuns in the convent where the artist was working; or in the famous whose faces have been painted into pictures. A comic anecdote arises from the Marquis of Mantua's criticism of a Saint Sebastian by Fran-cesco Monsignori:

'Francesco, you should have a good model to sit for that

saint.' The artist replied: 'I am copying a stalwart porter, who is what I want.' The Marquis added: 'The limbs of your saint are not true and do not show the fear of a man bound and shot at; if you will allow me, I will show you what you ought to do ... When you have bound your porter, send for me and I will show you how.' On the following day Francesco adopted this advice and sent secretly for the Marquis without however knowing his purpose. The Marquis came out as if infuriated holding a loaded crossbow, and ran to the model crying aloud, 'Traitor you are a dead man, but I have caught you as I wished,' and similar things, on hearing which the porter gave himself up for lost and tried to break the ropes, his contortions showing the fear of a man who expects to be shot, and the horror of death ... By this means the painter was enabled to give his picture the utmost perfection.[10]

The Renaissance established the precedent that serious art treatises did not talk of models. After Vasari, the two types of writing about models kept to their own books. Mindful of this, when the English began to write about their developing national art in the eighteenth century, they made sure they echoed the serious manner in which the Renaissance theorists expressed themselves.

Jonathan Richardson's aesthetic principles in the early eighteenth century could not be closer to those of the fifteenth-century Italians when he writes that

> In order to follow nature exactly, a man must be well acquainted with nature, and have a reasonable knowledge of geometry, proportion (which must be varied according to the sex, age and quality of the person), anatomy, osteology and perspective.[11]

And in sneering reference to those

> who have wrote of painting, in describing the works of painters in their lives, or on other occasions, have very rarely done any more; or in order to give us a great idea of some of the best painters, have told us such silly stories,[12]

he also could not be closer to the Italians in the style in which he chooses to express those principles. Because his is a work of theory, the model is not allowed into it. Richardson goes so far in playing down the model's importance that he tries to deny that they are needed at all. He approvingly tells of the Bolognese nobleman who asked a painter if he could see the model for his female heads:

> 'I will show you,' said Guido . . . so he called his colour grinder, a great greasy fellow, with a brutal look like the devil, and bade him sit down, and turn his head and look up to the sky; and then taking his chalk, drew a Magdalen after him, exactly in the same view and attitude, and same lights and shadows, but as handsome as an angel. The Count thought it was done by enchantment. 'No,' said Guido, 'my dear Count, but tell your painter that the beautiful and pure idea must be in the head, and then it is no matter what the model is.'[13]

This unwillingness on the part of serious writers to deal with the model continues today. The lightweight books have done such a successful job of aversion therapy that scholars have been permanently scared off the subject, terrified at getting mixed up with the personality and biographical side of art history. They regard such interest as the province of the gossip columnist and, as such, beneath the notice of in-depth reporters like themselves.

The only ways they can cope with models are by naming them or ignoring them. Naming names — what could be called the Victorine Meurend syndrome — leads them to identify the model's name with the pleasure that comes from stating a fact. Anyone reading about Manet learns the name of Victorine Meurend. But knowing the name of the model for *l'Olympia* and *Déjeuner sur l'herbe* has as little effect on the viewer's understanding of these paintings as knowing what colour trousers Manet wore when painting them.

Kenneth Clark ignores them. Unfortunately, his rush to back off from the inspirational model myth has landed him straight in the arms of another myth, that of the artist as creator. In *The Nude* the model is excluded firmly from his scheme of things: 'This is the type of female nude which was to dominate Venetian art for a century, and through Dürer, greatly to influence the physical ideal of Germany; and it seems reasonable to attribute its invention to Giorgione ...[14] The notion of the male artist's invention, which swells up on occasion into the more imposing notion of the male artist's creation, occurs frequently in *The Nude*. He credits Rubens with creating 'A new complete race of women ... He takes the female body, the plump, comfortably clothed female body of the north, and transforms it imaginatively with less sacrifice of its carnal reality than had ever been necessary before.'[15] The idea of Rubens creating a race fits nicely with the God-like attributes of the artist but it ignores the help he must have had from his model.

Models lose out whether they are treated in terms of anecdote or in terms of theory. If they are mentioned in connection with theory they are seen as little more than tools for gaining the necessary skills, an approach which dehumanizes them on a personal level and denies information on a professional one. Information about the hours, class, pay and sex of the group of models whose shadow hovers over Vasari's *Lives*, the nude models from whom it is recommended the artists learn to draw, is not to be had. Vasari lacks all interest in the life of the everyday model, the one who enabled the avant-garde Renaissance artists to improve their skills, and he has no conception that details of such a life could be of interest to anyone else.

It is possible to construct a general picture of modelling from the Renaissance theorists and the less chatty bits of the classical writers, but it takes a great deal of reading between the lines and there is no absolute certainty that the conclusion reached is the right one. Modern scholarship has convinced itself, in *The Oxford Companion to Art*, for example, that the presence of naked athletes in the gynmnasia made models unnecessary in classical Greece. Yet the picture which emerges from the classical writers of a flourishing art industry with an aesthetic of tidied-up likeness to life, suggests it is unlikely that any art devoted to representations of the beautiful body would be able to function without models for the artist to call on when necessary. Xenophon reports that Socrates asked the sculptor Cleiton how he produced the illusion of life in his statues of runners, wrestlers, boxers and fighters:

> 'Is it,' he added, 'by faithfully representing the form of living beings that you make your statues look as if they had lived?'
> 'Undoubtedly.'
> 'Then is it not by accurately representing the different parts of the body as they are affected by the pose — the flesh wrinkled or tense, the limbs compressed or outstretched, the muscles taut or loose — that you make them look more like real members and more convincing?'
> 'Yes, certainly.'[16]

That wrinkled flesh and those taut muscles imply the existence of a model standing for hours in front of a sculptor — an activity more likely to be allotted to slaves than athletes. Sketches could have been made from athletes and then others brought in for the tedious business of posing. The process was perhaps not unlike that practised by Leonardo who recommended noting people in action — nude bathers at the baths, for example — but had models pose as reminders later.

It is probable that modelling in the classical world was a two-tier affair. The modelling aristocrats were the beautiful individuals, the men and women admired for bodies which approached the perfection which the Greeks strove to embody in their art. Athenaeus says that Lais was so lovely painters copied her bosom and breasts and Phryne so beautiful that Apelles painted her as Venus Anadyomene and Praxiteles sculpted her as the Cnidian Venus.[17] Then came less glamorous models, some of whom perhaps, as in eighteenth-century England, were reknowned for one particularly fine feature. Xenophon says that since it was unlikely that any one model could embody the beauty that it was art's task to give form to, the painter Parrhasius combined the most beautiful details of several.[18]

The self-sufficiency of the medieval and early Renaissance studio system, in which the craft of painting was handed down via apprentices, makes it seem unlikely that anyone from the outside would be brought in to model. Far more likely, as a note by Leonardo da Vinci suggests, that an apprentice would take up whatever pose was needed.[19] There are drawings of young men done by Pollaiuolo's circle which suggest that apprentices modelled — for women, too, when necessary, since the church frowned on women modelling. But who modelled for Pisanello's delicate drawings of women done in the early fifteenth century?

Though the modelling profession developed from the Renaissance conviction that drawing from life was the basis of artistic skill, a belief which was subsequently institutionalized in the academies of art, the theoretical writings give no clues as to whether the models were paid, whether modelling was a full-time profession, or how early women began to model. There are hints that from the late fifteenth century artists were developing an idea of the good model. Leonardo da Vinci offers advice on improving one's drawing which suggests selecting 'some one who is well grown and who has not been brought up in doublets, and so may not be of stiff carriage, and make him go through a number of agile and graceful actions'.[20] It is a fascinating adumbration of Poynter's nineteenth-century praise of Italians for their beautiful feet unmarked by English shoes.

Paradoxically, the detailed anecdotes are no more revealing, for if the theoretical writings reduce models to materials like paper and pens, the anecdotal writings distort them by chronicling the atypical. How frequent was it for an artist to run away with his model as Fra Filippo Lippi did? Probably not very, yet it is this type of story, included by Vasari for its rarity value, that has helped form the notion of the normal in artist-model relationships.

While the theoretical writings freeze questions at source, the anecdotes raise more questions than they answer. The Francesco Monsignori story alone suggests several. How common was it for a porter to sit for a painter? Would only a lower-class man model nude? Would he expect a reward for his work? Does the fact that he is a porter mean that professional models did not exist in fifteenth-century Italy or was the artist merely exercising his time-honoured prerogative of selecting the best body for his purpose?

Since scholarship has ignored them and theoretical writings seen them in terms akin to drawing aids, models have been left to the mercies of the lighter literature. The lack of attempts to piece together an account of modelling is a direct result of the ways of writing about the model who is neither to be taken seriously (low writing) or acknowledged (high writing). Because of this division, the fantasies have flourished and models' history is a mystery. For what else is it but fantasy to see every model as nude and female? And what else but myth when anecdote after anecdote dwells on the sexual relationship between a male painter and a female model not just in the past, when more men were artists than women, but even today when half the student intake of art schools is female?

Notes

1   C.J. Bulliet, *The Courtezan Olympia* (New York, 1930), p. 85 and p. 162.
2   Angelo S. Rappoport, *Famous Artists and Their Models* (London, 1913), pp. 129-30.
3   Bulliet, *Courtezan Olympia*, p. 84.
4   Anthony Blunt, *Artistic Theory in Italy* (Oxford, 1940).
5   Edmond and Jules de Goncourt, *Manette Salomon*, 1866 (Paris, 1896), ch. 8.
6   Leonardo Battista Alberti, *On Painting* (Yale University Press, 1971), Book 2, p. 65.
7   Ibid., Book 3, p. 93.
8   Ibid., Book 3, pp. 93-4.
9   Carlo Pedretti, *Leonardo da Vinci On Painting: A Lost Book* (Peter Owen, 1965), pp. 78-9.
10 Giorgio Vasari, *Lives of Painters, Sculptors and Architects*, ed., W. Gaunt (4 vols., Dent, 1963), vol. 3, p. 37.
11 Jonathan Richardson, *The Works of Mr. Jonathan Richardson* (London, 1773), 'Essay on the Theory of Painting', p. 79.
12 Ibid., 'Essay on the Art of Criticism', p. 177.
13 Ibid., 'Essay on the Theory of Painting', p. 96.
14 Kenneth Clark, *The Nude*, 1956 (Pelican, 1980), p. 117.
15 Ibid., p. 137.
16 Xenophon, *Memorabilia*, Book 3, ch. 10.
17 Athenaeus, *The Deipnosophists*, Book 13.
18 Xenophon, *Memorabilia*, Book 3, ch. 10.
19 Jean Paul Richter, *The Literary Works of Leonardo da Vinci*, (2 vols., Oxford University Press, 1939), vol. 2, section 1454.
20 Ibid., vol. 1 section 497.

8
The Propagation of the Myth

From Xenophon to Augustus John, writers have presented the female model in terms of the titillating anecdote, and it is these accessible and entertaining tales of sex in the studio which have helped form the notion of the artist's model in use today.

It is impossible to see this emphasis on the sexual side of the female model as anything but a product of the masculine mind. Even in times when male models played a more important role in artistic life than they do today, more interest, curiosity and excitement was roused by the female model. It is not that the naughty model does not exist. Merely that the way she eclipses all other models is less a reflection of the truth than a reflection of male excitement at this particular element of the artist-model relationship.

A problem of assembling facts about modelling in the classical world is that for the writers models do not exist unless they are female, beautiful, and have a bit of scandal attached to their names with which the author can regale his readers. Nearly every reference to a specific model by a classical writer is to a female model. Quiet as clams about the identity of male models, they shout out the names of the women who pose. Even Xenophon, born in the fifth century BC, talks in the *Memorabilia* of the artists who came to paint Theodota's portrait and as much as decency allowed her to show; a remarkable reference given that the art historian is yet to be born who would claim that the Greeks were as interested in the female as the male nude until well into the fourth century BC. (For good measure, he adds that 'she was ready to keep company with anyone who pleased her'.)[1]

The Romans continued the tradition. In the first century BC, Marcus Tullius Cicero writes in *De Inventione* that when the inhabitants of Crotona asked Zeuxis for a temple painting of Juno, he asked them in return for their most beautiful young girls. He chose five, combining their best features in his painting.[2] There are three anecdotes involving female models and immorality in Pliny's *Natural History* of the first century AD. Arellius

> profaned the art by a disgraceful bit of profanity; for, being always in love with some woman or other, it was his practice in painting goddesses, to give them the features of his mistresses; hence it is, that there were always some figures of prostitutes to be seen in his pictures.[3]

Apelles fell in love with Alexander the Great's mistress while painting her nude portrait, upon which Alexander gave her to him as a gift.[4] Zeuxis inspected naked maidens of Agrigentum (the same story as Cicero had placed at Crotona) to find the perfect body for his painting, finally selecting five of them.[5] In addition to describing how Phryne was painted by Apelles and sculpted by Praxiteles, Athenaeus in the second century AD tells how she was acquitted from a capital charge by displaying her bosom. The judges found her body so goddess-like they were afraid to condemn her to death.[6] None of these stories is as innocent as it appears. In the Zeuxis story a thrill comes from the thought of the virgins revealing their pristine bodies to the raking eyes of the artist. In the Arellius story the model's immorality is perversely emphasized by associating her sexual knowledge with the divinities she poses for. (This association of like with unlike is not unusual in model stories. While Pliny is amused by the idea of harlots posing for goddesses, Vasari is amused by Leonardo da Vinci considering using a prior he disliked as the model for Judas in *The Last Judgement*.)[7]

These examples, and others like them, established the prurient way in which the female model was seen and still is seen today. Some of these stories which first saw the light of day in pre-Christian times have never been allowed to die. Zeuxis and the maidens is an instance. Cicero, Pliny, Alberti and Vasari are among those who used it; and in eighteenth-century England, several writers repeat it to give classical authority to their belief that art should be an improvement on life.

It tends to be only the anecdotes about female models which get passed down the ages. The Zeuxis story is not the only classical tale which recommends creating the ideal body from several bodies. There is Xenophon's account of Parrhasius combining the most beautiful details of several bodies to arrive at perfection. But the Parrhasius story has a drawback: it is unclear whether the models are male or female and even serious-minded writers of theory prefer their model stories to be about women.

The classical writers' references to copying athletes, the Renaissance theorists' belief that the male body was the best from which to learn to draw, Vasari's story of the model for St Sebastian and the comic model stories in Victorian artists' autobiographies are evidence that though the female model was written about in a manner heavy with sexual innuendo, the male model was not ignored. His disappearance from the literature occurred when Bohemia's stress on the male artist-female model relationship gave rise to a new category of books about artists and their mistress-models. (The St Sebastian model has disappeared from the Penguin abridged Vasari *Lives* because the artist in whose story he appears is no longer known today.)

The common factor of this new type of book is the belief that the pairing of a male artist and a female model is of such inbuilt interest that all that is necessary to prepare it for publication is a sprinkling of such words as sex, nude, inspiration and masterpiece. The variations come not from their content but from the arguments used to justify it.

Dr Angelo S. Rappoport's *Famous Artists and Their Models* appeared in 1913, within memory of nineteenth-century anxiety over models, and so before he gets under way with the mandatory catalogue of artist-model couples he takes pains to dispel any lingering Victorian prudishness that might surround the subject by arguing for it as a proper one.

Rappoport justifies nudity on the grounds of its idealism: 'I shall even go so far as to say that nudity in art may elevate the mind, for it glorifies the perfection of the body, paradoxical as that may sound.'[8] He attacks the idea that life classes are centres of orgiastic scenes and attacks those 'virtuous prudes' who think that because a woman has modelled she must be immoral. Rappoport feels that such accusations are insults against the artist whose works have given such pure aesthetic and intellectual pleasure and against the models who have 'in some respects a right to share in the glory and admiration of the masters'.[9] His defence is that

> since the days of antiquity their beauty has inspired the creative artistic genius; the contemplation of their perfect bodies, their harmonious lines, their matchless forms has enabled painters and sculptors of all ages to give reality to their ideal conceptions.[10]

His strategy is to make the models appear as respectable as the matrons who despise them. Many 'support with their earnings old parents, orphaned sisters and brothers, or their own little ones'. They 'pose for one artist only, who rarely uses another model' and many 'refuse to undress before the artist's eyes since that is too like a man and woman facing each other and not an artist gazing upon a model'.[11] He spends so much time arguing against the charges of immorality flung at models one wonders why he chose to write about them in the first place. But write he does. The apologies over, he launches into the familiar litany which runs from Praxiteles and Phryne to Goya and the Duchess of Alba.

While Rappoport was still fighting the hangover caused by an excess of nineteenth-century prudishness, C.J. Bulliet writing *The Courtezan Olympia* in 1930 comes across as a true interwar man, aware of Freud, fascinated by free love, determined not to mince the dirty words of what can only be called, with apologies to the nineteenth-century's hearty muscular Christians, muscular sexuality. The book's beginning is positively bracing:

> This is a book of art and of sin. It is a panorama, through the ages, of artists and their mistresses — fair women who have unclothed their bodies as models, but who, more important, have had the eager feminine vitality — the vitality that burns, the eagerness that bites — to inspire

creative energy.[12]

Where Rappoport attempts to make his models equal married women in respectability, Bulliet suggests that family life is inimical to the production of great art:

> The influence of a faithful wife or a devoted mother or an anxious sister is peculiarly vicious. She is afraid of genius — jealous — fearful it will break the bonds in which she holds her man. Even the mistress is salutory only so long as she has the zest of her unconventionality — only so long as she senses the trend of her lover's inspiration and seeks to lure him on and on to accomplishment. The time generally comes when she, too, grows afraid of the monstrosity she has helped shape, and then she seeks to curb its further growth.[13]

Bulliet classifies artists according to their attitude to social conventions. Artists like Van Gogh become unhinged by the conflict between genius and morals. Raphael, Apelles, Goya, Renoir and Rodin, he claims, are 'hardier, healthier souls, pagans who recognise the impulses of their bodies, who are not ashamed nor afraid of either, and who have dared confess with brush and chisel the frankly libertine-prostitute mainspring of their art'. Other less dashing artists conform outwardly to the conventions by having a wife at home for child-bearing and a model in the studio 'for soul inspiration' and also for bodily stimulation unless she happens to be 'hymeneally virtuous' or a patron's property, when a lesser model will have to service that need.[14]

It is impossible to avoid the feeling that though Bulliet's book is ostensibly about models, its real heroes are the artists whose genius 'is as wise instinctively as God, and like God refuses steadfastly to create according to the dictates of morals'. Bulliet loves these lusty creators who know that sex and creativity are linked: 'Slime and loam are the hotbeds of creation — deodorants and disinfectants kill the vital germs.'[15]

In 1972, Muriel Segal's *Dolly On the Dias: The Artist's Model in Perspective* was published. Despite its breathless tone, the book seems flatter than its predecessors, maybe because the author writing in the sexually tolerant seventies has no cause to battle for, no necessity to prove the morality of modelling, no deep belief in the sexual source of great art. But the pattern remains the same: an account of artists and their models through the ages. A selection of chapter titles gives the bias of the book: 'Phryne. Too sexy for a deity', 'Lucrezia and Spinetta Buti. The runaway nuns who became best-selling virgins', 'Mona Lisa. Her trials and tribulations in Leonardo's studio', 'Henrickje Stoffels. The servant who was model, mistress and manageress to Rembrandt'.[16]

All these books share a core of famous artists who have painted or sculpted the female and round whom cling hints of relationships with women: Apelles, Praxiteles, Raphael, Rubens, Titian, Manet. Sexual relationships are claimed by authors even where the evidence is doubtful, and the models behind the painted images are named on the shakiest of assumptions.

There are no male models in these books because they would complicate the presentation of the Bohemian artist and his lusty model. Nor is there any homosexuality. When Rappoport discusses Michelangelo it is to describe the Platonic love he bore Vittoria Colonna at the end of his life:

> Michelangelo, the chaste and austere, was not swayed in his artistic production by passion and sensual emotions; indeed carnal desires were almost strangers to his nature. The only love Michelangelo knew was such as would have delighted the soul of Plato himself, for it was spiritual, chaste, noble, free from gross desire and cravings of the flesh, and platonic in every sense of the world. Whilst the majority of people, when speaking of love, only mean desire, Michelangelo really loved.[17]

It is unlikely that the only love Michelangelo knew was free from gross desire, but the claim is evidence of a determined desire to see all artists as heterosexual. The lack of curiosity about Michelangelo's male models is further proof of the feeling discussed in chapter 1 that there is something God-given about the male artist-female model relationship.

The earlier writers' excited reaction to the female model, and the recent Bohemian view of the female model-male artist relationship show a remarkable continuity. Taken together they reveal some definite patterns in the way women models have been written about. These patterns have recurred with such regularity they qualify as model myths.

There is the sexually willing model who makes love to the artist. Benvenuto Cellini's autobiography written in the mid sixteenth century sets the tone: 'It happened as was natural at the age of twenty-nine that I had taken into my service a girl of great beauty and grace, whom I used as a model in my art, and who was also complaisant of her personal favours to me.'[18] Four hundred years later, Jean-Paul Crespelle in *Picasso and his Women* writes of Fernande Olivier: 'In those days it was also part of a model's duties to satisfy her employer's physical needs.'[19]

There is the beautiful model who inspired the artist to great works. Phryne seen by Praxiteles wading into the sea during a festival is an example from fourth-century Greece.[20] In this century, Augustus John has been written of by his biographer Michael Holroyd in similar terms: 'Alick Scheperler's face and figure could summon from him great art.'[21]

There is the model who goes outside the normal social laws as in Vasari's account of Fra Filippo Lippi's convent girl who ran off with him to be his model and wife, and Goya's maja who supposedly posed for him nude. The twentieth-century counterparts are the society ladies who it is said posed only too willingly for the renowned Rodin, tearing off their clothes as they crossed the threshold of his studio — women, all of them, who threw off conventional society in exchange for *la vie de bohème*.

The effect of these myths has been to take models out of their historical context. The difference is blurred between Theodota in classical Greece and the Duchess of Alba in eighteenth-century Spain. Creation, passion, notoriety are all, and history does not come into it. In all these stories, modelling is reduced to a burning relationship between a male artist and a female model. Similarities rather than differences are focused upon and inconvenient facts that might complicate the exciting picture of the artist and his mistress-model ignored.

The unchallenged reign of the myths has made the model's attributes of femininity and sexuality the norm. The rude nude female model has become a cliché for our times, a symbol which lends itself innocently to the pages of *Punch* or less decorously to the 'model' sign next to prostitutes' doorbells.

The sexual meaning of model has become so commonplace since the Second World War that even respectable writers can use it without risking their reputations. One who did was William Russell Flint, a Royal Academician who made his name and his money from watercolours of semi-nude ladies. According to reports he was a shy married man whose relationships with his models were highly professional, yet in 1951 he published *Models of Propriety*, a money-making exercise whose mildly naughty illustrations were accompanied by a mildly naughty text.

His biographer says that Flint dreamed of writing about the atmosphere of mutual trust and companionship between great artists and their models, but this book hardly furthers that aim. He begins with Rosina Dumplington, 'Because she does not pose for the nude, thus presenting, as it were, an armoured front against critical assault.' He concurs with the Victorian view of modelling as a Descent, which must have infuriated the models who worked for him. He talks of models who disappear for weekends with men and describes Miss Eugenia Meeker who opened the door to the 'coffee bearing menial stark naked', causing the maid to scream and flee. He tells of Miss Leonora Welworthy who, beaten on the bottom with a tawse for posing nude, shows her stripes to the painter, who, in a word picture of politest pornography, was 'distracted and helpless between his love of classical perfection and burning indignation at the thought of his lovely model being ignominiously and painfully whipped and her English curves temporarily marred by Scottish thongs . . .'[22]

Etc. etc. is all one can say. Meant to amuse, the book's real lesson is that William Russel Flint RA saw no stigma in associating himself with this world of sex in the studio, proof beyond doubt that the model had become a sign for acceptable naughty nudity.

Aside from the connotations of sex and selling one's body which have always clung to female modelling, two late-nineteenth-century developments ensured that it was the model, and not, for example, the chorus girl, whose name has emerged today as a code word for prostitute.

The first of these was the *tableaux vivants* craze of the 1890s in which young women in flesh-coloured tights posed on the music-hall stage as living representations of famous paintings. These living pictures were the beginning of a chain that included the show girls standing still as statues (prosecutions would have resulted if they had moved) at the wartime Windmill Theatre in London's Soho and continues today in strip show set-pieces.

The second development was the trade from the 1880s in selling photographs as aids to painters through the fine art press. A typical advertisement by Erdmann and Schanz offers photographs of

> Paris salon pictures, classical undraped figures, secular and religious subjects, statuary, views, yachts, actresses, heads, portraits, artists' life studies (including the celebrated series by Gloeden), children, eastern types, animals, flowers, fruit, clouds, waves, rustic scenes.

Despite the variety of subjects, only the Paris salon pictures are illustrated and both these are of female nude figures. Vigée-Lebrun's *Peace Leading Abundance* has an allegorical excuse for Abundance's bare breasts, but Chantron's *Water Flower* of a full-length nude woman has no classical or allegorical justification for her lack of clothes.

Both developments brought fine art nudity down to earth. With the living pictures and fine art photographs offering nudity under an artistic umbrella, the peculiarly twentieth-century link of photography, pin-ups and fine art was established. In affluent Western countries magazines with the word art or artists in the title turn out on inspection to be nothing more than a collection of nude or nearly nude ladies sheltering under the respectable cloak of art. An American magazine of the 1920s, *Artists and Models*, specialized in a mixture of photographs of flimsily clad chorus girls from Broadway shows with reproductions of much nuder Paris Salon paintings with names like *Morning*, or *Venus in her Car*, but there is nothing about artists or models in the text. A magazine from England of the 1950s, *The Art Advertiser and Studio News*, is illustrated with half-naked pin-ups whose come-hither glances belie the art and news aspects of its title.

The magazine's most entertaining feature is the pretence that art is the subject and artists the readers. An article entitled 'Giacometti — Artist with a Mission' carries no picture of his work since, as the text makes clear, there is no work by this artist which could interest its readers:

From our point of view the effort does not appear to be worth while. His nudes are skinny things with small heads; men with matchstick torsoes and women with not one vital statistic.

But Giacometti is a man with a mission — with a mission to discover 'how thin the human body can be and still exist'.[23]

But it is not the editorial sections but the advertisements which expose the line that goes from artist's model via 'art' photography and posing to prostitution. The modern counterparts of the nineteenth-century photographic firms drop the animals, flowers and rustic scenes which their predecessors offered (even if they did not choose to illustrate them); they offer instead 'Fine art figure studies, pin ups, classical nudes, and every type of glamour photograph of the world's most beautiful girls supplied for artists and bona fide collectors.' The last words add an aura of respectability though it is unlikely that firms checked potential customers for serious intentions.

The copy for a club billed as London's newest photographic studio runs:

Visitors interested in photography welcome as guests. Spacious lounge where models can relax in pleasant surroundings and enjoy good coffee and chat with Ken's wife whilst waiting to go on modelling appointments at the many other studios.

Photographers can use this club to keep in touch with models, or may bring their own models to this well-equipped photographic studio. Our resident models always available.

Amateurs are well catered for at the most reasonable price with full use of studio props, drapes for figure, glamour, pin-up, and flashlight photography under the expert guidance of Ken . . .who runs the club.[24]

Substitute Madam for Ken's wife, clients for photographers and prostitutes for models and the club's respectable façade slips somewhat.

The classified advertisements make it clear that there is no way in which the models mentioned in its columns can be mistaken for the clothes model who embodied the generally accepted meaning of model by this time.

Wanted — attractive, well-developed young lady model, willing to visit occasionally for posings. Agreed expenses.

Model aged 20-27 for Saturday and Sunday afternoon painting sessions. London area, pose in own room if convenient. International prizewinning painter aged 35, pays usual fees.

It is to this role of private posing in the nude that prostitutes refer when they put 'model' by their doorbells.

The model's other twentieth-century attribute, her femininity, can be traced through the press. With the advent of Bohemia at the end of the nineteenth century, newspapers and periodicals in England began to lose interest in the male model. An article in *The Bohemian* of December 1893 called 'Artists Models of Modern Babylon' admitted both sexes into its account, but only got down to enthusiastic details when discussing the women:

Although I shall make every endeavour to give an adequate account of the male section of this body, I have every reason to believe that more is conjectured, less is known, and a keener interest is taken in the female element, and accordingly it is assuredly my duty to satisfy the preponderating curiosity.

The author presents an appetizing picture of the female model: 'Picture to yourself a good-looking, graceful, good-figured, fresh-coloured, small-footed, pretty-handed, tastefully-dressed maiden and you will see, not an ideal model, but one of everyday occurrence.'

Though journalistic conventions of the period forbade the mention of nude modelling, specialist magazines could evade this restriction. An article called 'A Plea for the Artist's Model' which appeared in *The Art Chronicle* of 23 April 1910, was illustrated by a rear view of a standing female nude model, a photograph which carried a most elevating caption, 'A model posed to illustrate Hogarth's line of beauty.' Written to announce the formation of a model's register to be kept in the magazine's office, the article concentrated its discussion on female models, informing readers that 'eminent ladies have posed as artists' models, ladies whose names are above suspicion and households words'. While admitting that 'on the face of it, there appears to be some difficulties' in the way of respectable young women submitting to the indignity of sitting as models to painters of the opposite sex, it claimed somewhat opaquely that 'the very factor of her reputation being so assailable is her best protection' and explained that 'the absolute necessity of painting from nature cannot be understood except by those who practice the art'.

Between the two world wars, articles about models were a way of inserting a mild cheesecake element into a respectable publication. *Picture Post* in the thirties ran one feature each week showing scantily dressed women, always, of course, justified with a news or general interest angle. The most common subject was fashion, with an emphasis on swimsuits, underwear and lowcut evening gowns, but showgirls, sometimes in backstage undress, were popular, too.

On 28 January 1939, 'Day in the Life of an Artist's Model' filled the slot. Thirteen photographs over two double-page spreads are supported by an informative 800-word text by Robert Burnett. The subject, 'Green-eyed auburn-haired Freda Walker' with measurements of 32, 25, 36 and 'a strong 13-inch calf' (since classical times spindly-legged nudes have not appealed to artists on the grounds of unsightly top-heaviness) is a professional model who exercises, wears sensible shoes to avoid deforming her feet and goes to bed early to keep in trim. The pictures are equally informative. Three show her modelling, one resting in a dressing gown between sittings, one on her way to an appointment, and four off duty, shopping or relaxing at home in the evening. There are also three pictures of works she modelled for, among them L. Glasson's bare-breasted *The Young Rower* which fascinated visitors to the Thirties Exhibition held in 1979 in London's Hayward Gallery (Rochdale Art Gallery).

The article's documentary approach hides the fact that choices have been made. The model did not have to be young, or pretty or even female. And two of the three largest pictures — half-page plates both of them — did not have to show her modelling in the nude. Not frontal nudity of course: the thirties code of censorship frowned on breasts in photographs in family magazines. Just her back, bottom and legs, in exactly the same pose *The Art Chronicle* used in 1910. Since one of the examples of the painted Freda, a three-quarter length portrait by T.C. Dugdale, shows her in a dress, she was clearly not only a nude model. Yet it is this aspect of modelling which the editor has helped shore up by his choice of photographs.

Forty years later, on 12 May 1980, the *Guardian*'s Polly Toynbee interviewed Yvonne Vinall, a professional female model in her forties who works for some well-known artists and at some well-known art schools, and described her at work. Two photographs accompany the article: a small clothed one of Mrs Vinall against a painting of herself by Peter Johns, and a large photograph showing her modelling nude, but distanced by having her viewed through the students' heads and their paintings of her. The article is top quality Toynbee, level, informative and dedicated to letting Mrs Vinall tell her own story. As with Freda Walker a photo is shown which proves that not all artists painted Mrs Vinall in the nude. Yet the combination of the larger of the two photos and the five-column heading in black type reading 'The hard grey afternoon light shone down cruelly on her skin. All those wrinkles and imperfections the weaknesses of almost any naked body, came under harsh scrutiny' give the opposite impression. Once again, fascination with the idea of a woman removing her clothes in front of staring eyes had led to a masking of the fact that modelling is neither exclusively nude or exclusively female.

In November 1980, *The Sunday Times* magazine ran a feature on objects, services and people for hire. Yvonne Vinall turned up again, illustrating the artist's model in full frontal nudity. Newspapers are not wrong in illustrating their articles with female nude models. Their subjects earn a living by being precisely that. The distortion occurs because they are presented as only modelling nude, as the only sex which models nude, and as the only sex which models. At least the *Guardian* story refers to a male model; most articles do not mention men at all. They may be in a minority but they do exist, whatever the anecdotes, books and articles would have us believe.

Notes

1 Xenophon, *Memorabilia*, Book 3, ch. 11.
2 Marcus Tullius Cicero, *De Inventione*, II, I, i.
3 Gaius Plinius Secundus, *Natural History*, Book 35, ch. 37.
4 Ibid., ch. 36.
5 Ibid., ch. 36.
6 Athenaeus, *Deipnosophists*, Book 13, ch. 59.
7 Giorgio Vasari, *Lives of Painters, Sculptors and Architects*, ed., W. Gaunt (4 vols., Dent, 1963), vol. 2, p. 161.
8 Angelo S. Rappoport, *Famous Artists and Their Models* (London, 1913), p. 16.
9 Ibid., p. 4.
10 Ibid., p. 4.
11 Ibid., p. 8.
12 C.J. Bulliet, *The Courtezan Olympia* (New York, 1930), p. 1.
13 Ibid., p. 4.
14 Ibid., pp. 3, 4.
15 Ibid., p. 1.
16 Muriel Segal, *Dolly on the Dais: The Artist's Model in Perspective* (Gentry Books, 1972).
17 Rappoport, *Famous Artists*, p. 93.
18 Benvenuto Cellini, *The Life of Benvenuto Cellini* (Phaidon, 1949), Book First, p. 100.
19 Jean-Paul Crespelle, *Picasso and His Women* (Hodder and Stoughton, 1969), p. 51.
20 Athenaeus, *Deipnosophists*, Book 13, ch. 60.
21 Michael Holroyd, *Augustus John*, 1974, (Penguin, 1976), p. 281.
22 W. Russell Flint, *Models of Propriety* (Michael Joseph, 1951), p. 30.

23   *The Art Advertiser and Studio News*, vol. 1, no. 7, p. 8.
24   Ibid., vol. 2, no. 1.

9
The Model in Fiction

Artists' models are a rare breed of fictional character. There are few English novels in which they rise above bit player to featured role, and fewer still in which they star. When they do appear, they tend to be females and have a lot in common.

One reason for their infrequent fictional appearance is their relatively unimportant role in English life. But the main reason is that the elements of the stereotype which authors have accepted, models as female, sexually lax, outside conventional society and lower class, disqualified them for a sympathetic fictional treatment. These elements, give or take a characteristic or two — models' low status in the nineteenth century, their brainlessness in the twentieth — turn up repeatedly in the fiction of the last hundred and fifty years.

Male models' fictional appearances though rare are more varied. Saved from the sexual taint which clings to the female models and limits the roles in which they can be cast, the men are used more imaginatively. The stereotype of the comic male model who refuses to know his place has not inhibited authors from writing them other roles, though Gloucester, the male model in Weedon Grossmith's one-act play *A Commission* produced at Terry's Theatre in London in 1891, is a version of the comic male model familiar from *Punch* cartoons and artists' autobiographies. Based on life, Gloucester is made ridiculous by his familiar references to the Academicians of the day as Johnnie Millais and Teddy Poynter.

A different type of model appears in Oscar Wilde's short story *The Model Millionaire*, written at the same period as

A Commission. This model is a millionaire who takes it into his head to be painted as a beggar. A young visitor to the studio takes pity on his poverty and gives him half a guinea. Some days later, the young man receives a cheque for £10,000 from the model-millionaire which enables him to marry the girl he loves.[1]

In Nathaniel Hawthorne's *The Marble Faun* (1859) Miriam's model, as he is called, is part of the gothic strand of the novel and not its art side. Although he appears in Miriam's paintings dressed in peasant cloak and goatskin breeches like the figures who recline on the Spanish Steps waiting for artists 'to invite them within the magic realm of picture',[2] the role of Miriam's model is to further the spooky melodrama that is the subject of the book. The mystery of the possibly centuries-old model and his purpose in haunting Miriam is never, as is typical of so much of the mystery in this novel, satisfactorily solved. And the chance of exploring the sex role reversal in this artist-model relationship is never taken up.

Henry James's short story *The Real Thing*, which appeared in 1892, tells of the down-on-their-luck Major Monarch and his wife who try working as models but who turn out to be nowhere near as satisfactory as the professional models, the freckled cockney Miss Churm and the sallow little Italian, Oronte. The final irony, that the substitute is better than the real thing, emerges when Miss Churm and Oronte pose more convincingly for an aristocratic couple than the Monarchs who really are well-born.

Michael Innes's short story 'The Flight of Patroclus'[3] presents posing as a slip from conventional values. In his youth Lord Counterpoint, philanthropist and writer on social and moral questions, had posed nude with a society beauty of the period for a painting of Apollo pursuing Daphne. The picture had been cut up but has now been pieced together again and blackmail threatens.

In contrast to the treatment of male models, the spectacles of stereotype through which female models have been seen have blinded authors to the facts about them and blunted their imaginations as to their use in fiction. The stereotype has denied models a thoughtful and imaginative range of fictional roles and seen to it that the model is presented as a victim, or mildly criminal, or stupid or sluttish or as a fallen angel. It is hardly a positive image or even an interesting one.

The stereotype's tendency to blank out history has meant that novels have barely registered that models were important in the nineteenth century or that their importance diminished after the Second World War with the international acceptance of non-representational art and the replacement of the professional model by the part-time amateur. There are neither as many examples of the model in nineteenth-century fiction as might be expected in a century whose art was based on models, nor as few in this century whose art is not.

Even if authors wished to look past the stereotype to consider the female model, fictional conventions, particularly in the nineteenth century, saw to it that she was not allowed too interesting or important a role. Every single aspect of the stereotype disqualified her as fruitful Victorian heroine material. Sex above all was a difficult area for the nineteenth-century novel to deal with, particularly if it took place outside marriage, which was where models, almost by definition, were seen to stand. A female character who sexually transgressed had to suffer, and no character who started as bad had any hopes of fictional redemption. Lower-class origins were another drawback. Nineteenth-century heroines tend not to be from the working class. If they are, they are distanced from their background in some way, through education, grand ancestors or wealthy relatives, like Fanny Price in Jane Austen's *Mansfield Park* at the start of the century or Tess in Thomas Hardy's *Tess of the D'Urbervilles* at the end. It was a problem Arnold Bennett solved in his first published piece of fiction, a short story called *The Artist's Model* which appeared in *Titbits* in 1893 (and which, like the Henry James story of the previous year, had an artist needing models for his illustrations of an *édition de luxe* of a novelist's works), by having his poor but genteel model inherit £30,000 and a country house, thereby raising her status and enabling the artist she is to marry to get the three years rest he needs to save his failing eyesight.[4]

Though sexual activity and working-class origins did not exclude a character from a leading role in twentieth-century fiction, the elements of the stereotype which came into prominence after the First World War which made models brainless inhabitants of Bohemia whose role was to satisfy an artist sexually and inspire him artistically, seem to have been no more liberating to authors' imaginations than the nineteenth-century version they replaced.

A clever early use of the stereotype occurs in Chapter 10 of Bulwer-Lytton's *Lucretia or The Children of Night* (1846) in which the evil Gabriel learns to paint from the 'jovial, disorderly vagrant dog of a painter', his uncle Tom Varney. The model's immorality is suggested by naming the kind of pictures she poses for — Galatea leered at by Polyphemus, and nude goddesses owing more 'to the Galleries of Drury than to the divine' — and her sensuality, by describing how when Gabriel finished sketching he 'with an impudent wink at the model, flung himself back on his chair, folded his arms . . . The model, whom Gabriel's wink had roused, half-flattered, half indignant for a moment, lapsed into a doze.' Having established her sexual availability through the paintings and her sensuality through the way she is roused like a cat by Gabriel's wink, the author can use her to show that however bad the model is, she is not nearly so bad as Gabriel. When Gabriel threatens to pull the studio canary's eyes out, she attacks him. In retaliation, he seizes a chair and 'regardless of the gallanteries due to the sex, sent it right against the model, who was shaking her fist at him'. It is hard to think of a profession which could have supplied an equally convincing example of degraded womanhood who yet retained an element of humanity. A prostitute was too raw a character for an early Victorian novel, while to suggest a servant's sensuality to a society which relied on them and kept them under its roof, would have been as disturbing as imagining one's children making love.[5]

'A figure more perfect never served for model to a sculptor' is how a respectable female character is described earlier in the book.[6] Though superficially it might seem as if for once modelling has a positive image, the key word is sculptor not model. As Richard Jenkyns has pointed out in *The Victorians and Ancient Greece*[7] busts in white marble carried a wealth of refined and cultured connotations, and it is this that puts the woman whose body could serve as a model for a sculptor on a higher plane than the model who poses for pot-boilers.

Bulwer-Lytton's presentation of the sleepy sluttish model

posed no problems of credibility for his audience. But when a nineteenth-century author decides to make a model his heroine then all kinds of problems arise. James Stanley Little's *Whose Wife Shall She Be?* is evidence that Bohemian notions from France were infiltrating the English art world, although the change from the book's announced title of *Barracks and Bohemia* shows that the familiar Trollopian formula was felt to be a safer selling bet than new-fangled artistic ideas. Ralph Sigh, painter and heir to 'one of the oldest and richest baronies of England' wishes to marry the nude model Grace Harland. She refuses on the grounds of the social injury she will cause him.[8] It is a situation which was to be repeated when Du Maurier published *Trilby* six years later. Like Du Maurier, Little displays an enlightened attitude towards modelling, which Ralph describes to Grace as a profession and its opponents as 'women who are jealous of your prerogatives and freedom; men who are envious of ours'.[8] Nevertheless the artist hero is not required to put his liberal ideas into practice by making Grace his wife. Grace's convenient death from consumption renders his liberalism academic and frees him to marry the upper-class Gwendoline Clayton. In this way the author managed to uphold the social barriers between models and conventional society while at the same time displaying newly modern attitudes towards nude modelling.

What must be the best-known novel with a model as heroine, George Du Maurier's *Trilby*, was published in 1894. It tells of the period he and a group of friends spent in the Paris of the 1850s. (For a discussion of who was based on who see Leonée Ormond's *George Du Maurier*, 1969.)

What makes the book so fascinating is that Du Maurier accepts the stereotype but insists on making a nude model his heroine despite it. In every single way, Trilby the beautiful Irish model with the angel's feet fits the stereotype: she is female, working class (on her mother's side; her father was a doctor), outside conventional society and sexually knowledgable. On the surface it seems extraordinary that Du Maurier should have taken on such unpromising heroine material when purity campaigners prowled and fiction punished its women for sex outside marriage. But it was also the period of growing interest in French-style Bohemia,

141

and it is this interest Du Maurier feeds with his novel.

Trilby is a wondrously original heroine: beautiful, healthy, tall, loving, amusing *and* she rolls her own cigarettes. Her story is equally unconventional. Having fallen in love with Little Billee and he with her, she refuses to marry him on the grounds of her inferior social position. Subsequently she is bad-mouthed, as the Americans say, by Little Billee's snobbish and conventional mother, she is hypnotized by Svengali into becoming the finest singer in the world, and she finally dies a magnificent Victorian death with Little Billee by her side and Little Billee's mother at her knees begging forgiveness for her role in preventing the marriage. Significantly while Du Maurier allows his heroine the dignity and happiness of a death among friends he could not bring himself to permit her entry into polite society by means of marriage.

Given that either loss of virginity or nude modelling spelt immorality to Victorian eyes and that both together spelled sinfulness of the most scarlet sort, Du Maurier has to work hard to whitewash his heroine. Her career of downward mobility is explained as starting as a laundress (a profession which English readers may have taken at face value but which in Paris had long signalled sexual availability), then coming to grief 'through her trust in a friend of her mother's (a master stroke this for winning sympathy to have her 'first false step' the result of bad advice from that icon of Victorian womanhood), then becoming a model. Though she is not a virgin, Du Maurier does his best and gives her 'A virginal heart, so little did she know of love's heartaches and raptures and torment and jealousies.' Far from enjoying her body, he explains that she is its victim: 'lovely female shapes are terrible complicators of the difficulties and dangers of this earthly life, especially for the owner, and more especially if she be a humble daughter of the people, poor and ignorant, of a yielding nature, too quick to love and trust'. To justify her profession, he dusts off the familiar argument of model as breadwinner: 'Then she became a model besides, and was able to support her little brother, whom she dearly loved.' And in what may be an early use of 'promiscuous' in a sexual sense he explains that 'she did not sit promiscuously to anybody who asked'. As well as arguing for her innocence, Du Maurier undermines the reader's resistance to her way of life by presenting the standard nineteenth-century nudity equals purity defence:

> And here it would not be amiss for me to state a fact well known to all painters and sculptors who have used the nude model (except a few shady pretenders, whose purity, not being of the right sort, has gone rank from too much watching), namely, that nothing is as chaste as nudity. Venus herself, as she drops her garments and steps on to the model-throne, leaves behind her every weapon in her armoury by which she can pierce to the grosser passions of man. The more perfect her unveiled beauty, the more keenly it appeals to his higher instincts. And where her beauty fails (as it almost always does somewhere in the Venuses who sit for hire), the failure is so lamentably conspicuous in the studio light — that Don Juan himself, who has not got to paint, were fain to hide his eyes in sorrow and disenchantment and fly to other climes.
>
> All beauty is sexless in the eyes of the artist at his work.

At this point Du Maurier so warms to his defence that he consumes the model in its flames:

> But I have worked from many female models in many countries, some of them the best of their kind. I have also, like Svengali, seen Taffy 'trying to get himself clean', either at home or in the swimming-bath of the Seine; and never a sitting woman among them all who could match for grace or finish or splendour of outward form that mighty Yorkshireman sitting in his tub, or sunning himself like Illyssus, at the Bains Henri Quatre, or taking his running header à la hussarde, off the spring-board at the Bains Deligny, with a group of wondering Frenchmen gathered round.[9]

It is typical of Du Maurier to argue his premise out of existence, but given that his apology for the female nude model appeared in a period of unease about the nude model, it is a forgivable defence and an understandable nervousness.

Du Maurier, sophisticated satirist of social manners, wants

it both ways. His urbanity tells him nude modelling and sexual experience do not automatically make a woman wicked, but his timidity in the face of the public inhibits him from claiming that purity and posing could be compatible. As Trilby dies a most affecting Victorian death, he has Mrs Bagot, Little Billee's mother, beg her forgiveness (with any other author one would suspect Bagot was a play on bigot): 'You've never been to blame in any way — I've long known it — I've been full of remorse! — Forgive me!' Yet at the same time he reminds us of Trilby's blacker side, describing Mrs Bagot as worshipping

> this fast-fading lily — for so she called her in her own mind — quite forgetting (or affecting to forget) on what very questionable soil the lily had been reared, and through what strange vicissitudes of evil and corruption it had managed to grow so tall and white and fragrant![10]

This habit of undercutting his own arguments reveals his inability to support his heroine wholeheartedly.

Trilby's part in the book begins as she sits confident and cross-legged on the model's throne rolling a cigarette and ends as she lies on a sick bed having *The Pilgrim's Progress* read to her. The suggestion of punishment is overpowering. Du Maurier wants her to realize how bad she has been and he does this by making her ashamed of her profession. Little Billee is horrified when he sees Trilby sitting nude to the students at Carrel's. When she realizes why — 'Could it possibly be that he was shocked at seeing her sitting there?'[11] — she bursts into tears. She has been educated into guilt and she shows she has learned society's values by explaining that she had begun sitting to artists as a child ('mamma made me'): 'It seemed as natural for me to sit as for a man. Now I see the awful difference.'[12] Linked with this realization is her confession of sexual sins:

> And I have done dreadful things besides, as you must know — as all the Quartier knows. Baratier and Besson; but not Durien, though people think so. Nobody else, I swear — except old Monseiur Penque at the beginning, who was Mama's friend.[13]

Du Maurier puts Trilby through some harrowing punishments and it is only at the end, when she is too weak to be a threat to the values of conventional society, that everyone begs her forgiveness. By means of this purgatorial journey through the book, Trilby atones for her fall from grace and attains a nun-like purity. Only then can she and Little Billee be reunited, for no longer a nude model, she is no longer a threat to the British middle classes. As Du Maurier explains, it is love of the brotherly variety that Little Billee now feels for the alluring outsider.

Twentieth-century presentations of the model are no more positive. Hetty Finch, the model in Gilbert Cannan's *Mendel* (1916) is the daughter of the owner of a Margate lodging-house where Mendel's family has stayed. One day she appears at the family's Whitechapel home with fourteen shillings and a desire to make her living as a model. Hetty is presented as Mendel's equal, an outsider as he is, poor but with something to offer: 'His talent, her body, were shining offerings with which they both emerged from the depths of the despised.'[14] After Hetty becomes Mendel's mistress, she begins to play a role in his life and in that of his artist friends. 'She was learning her trade as they were learning theirs', writes Cannan. She picks up the jargon of the Paris Café where the artists meet (Lawrence's Café de Pompadour in *Women in Love* and the real-life Café Royal in Piccadilly) and she devotes herself to the group:

When Hetty found Calthrop painting a self-portrait, she set her four boys painting self-portraits, and when she found the older men talking about the beauty of roofs and chimneys, the four were soon ecstatic about roofs and chimneys, and painting them without knowing how it had come about. She could feel what was in the air, and had no difficulty making them conform to it, so that they were successful even while they were students, and were talked of and discussed and approached by dealers as though they were persons of consequence. Their life was one long intoxication: money, praise, wine and debauchery went to their heads, and of all these excitants Mendel had the largest share, and found himself the equal even of Kessler, whose father was a millionaire soap-boiler. He attained an extraordinary skill at doing what was expected of him, and developed an instinct as sharp as Hetty's for the success of the moment after next.[15]

The disapproval is strong. Hetty's career management is seen as a bad thing. Mendel gets so high that

> Weldon, who was uncommonly shrewd, had begun to see the dangers of allowing Hetty Finch to arrange their affairs, and when on top of that, Mendel, drunk with freedom and success, began to take charge, he thought it time to secure himself and began to withdraw from their undertakings and adventures.[16]

It is from this point that Hetty's downfall into comfort but not respectability begins. Although in material terms hers is a success story, ending the book with far more than the fourteen shillings with which she began, emotionally she is punished. She gets pregnant, and though she has a flat and a car, she has no husband and the baby dies. It seems impossible for models to escape censure in fiction; even enlightened writers see the wages of modelling as misery.

Miss Thiselton the model who appears in the subplot of the much reprinted *Alice-for-Short*, published in 1907 but set in the 1860s, also shows the dark side of the stereotype. She represents the model as outsider, outside the rank into which she wants to marry and outside its code of conduct. It is early shown that her behaviour is on the shady side of honest. She sets her cap at Charles Heath, the artist hero, whom she tries to inveigle into marriage. Despite her 'almost' beauty ('slight obliquity of vision' on the minus side but two beautiful side faces and rippling hair on the plus) she is ultimately unsuccessful, so enabling readers to let out their breath as this mystery-cum-love story draws to a close with the hero's marriage to a more suitable woman. Like Hetty Finch, Miss Thiselton is a model who uses her looks to try to advance in a world whose doors are shut against her, one more version of the horrid spectre of the model charming her way into a good marriage which haunted the nineteenth and early twentieth centuries. Her profession lays her open to some arch authorial comments:

Miss Thiselton was that very common occurrence — a young woman in reduced circumstances, who would be thankful for sittings if it was quite clearly understood that she wasn't a model. She drew a sharp line at her neck and wrists and required a certificate of character from artists before she sat for them.[17]

Poor lady models. Disapproved of if they removed their clothes, sneered at for excessive gentility if they refused.

The stupidity of models is a strong element in the inter-war twentieth-century stereotype, and one which Margery Allingham picks up in her detective novel of 1934, *Death of a Ghost*. The novel has four models, all female as would be expected at this period of interest in the glamorous Bohemian model. Two of them are treated as people: Belle Darling, the widow of the artist John Lafcadio, because she has never posed professionally, and Lisa who was discovered by Lafcadio in Italy in 1884 but has left the stereotype behind by making the transition from principal model to cook in Belle Darling's household. The remaining two are stupid. The Botticelli-haired Rosa Rosa, wife of a painter who had to marry her to get her out of Italy, is naive, young and possesses, the author tells us, several of the perfect model's peculiarities, among them unbelievable stupidity: 'She had been trained not to think, lest her roving fancy should destroy the expression she was holding.'[18] Like all natural models, she moved very little 'and then only to drop from one attitude into another, which she held with remarkable faithfulness'.[19] The second model, the ageing Donna Beatrice, wears her hair in an outdated Gibson Girl style and is chiefly remarkable for her vanity. She talks at a party about the time she was likened to the Rokeby Venus in a Turkish bath: 'That's all there is to it, but it goes on for hours', says an observer.[20]

The novel bears all the signs of research: Allingham has Rosa Rosa related to a gangster with a store in Saffron Hill, the centre of London's Italian colony. Even so, the best the author comes up with in terms of her models' personalities is vanity and dullness. In her heyday, we are told, Lafcadio never allowed Donna Beatrice to open her mouth in his presence. A similar observation is made of John Bidlake and his model Jenny Smith in *Point Counterpoint* six years earlier:

> Incarnation of beauty, incarnation of stupidity and vulgarity. A goddess as long as she was naked, kept her mouth shut, or had it kept shut for her with kisses; but oh, when she opened it, when she put on her clothes, her frightful hats! He remembered the time he had taken her to Paris with him. He had to send her back after a week. 'You ought to be muzzled, Jenny,' he told her, and Jenny cried.[21]

It is obvious that Margery Allingham's research involved talking to artists not models, and that her tale of Lafcadio forbidding Donna Beatrice to talk was based, as was Huxley's, on Augustus John. It is noticeable that Mona, who pops in and out of Anthony Powell's sequence of novels *A Dance to the Music of Time* becomes less stupid as her career progresses from artist's model to photographic model to film star, and her marital status goes from upper-class Templar to intellectual Quiggin to aristocratic Erridge. Says the narrator in *At Lady Molly's* (1957) 'I noticed how much firmer, more ruthless, her personality had become since I had first met her as Templar's wife, when she had seemed a silly empty-headed, rather bad-tempered beauty.'[22]

One aspect of the stereotype all fictional models share is sex. It underlies such superficially different presentations as Bulwer-Lytton's sluttish model, the ambitious Hetty Finch who uses sex to advance her career, and Gully Jimson's recollections of his models in terms of soft flesh and sexual generosity in Joyce Cary's *The Horse's Mouth* of 1943. Everyone who models for Mendel sleeps with him, not just Hetty who makes love to Mendel on their first meeting, but Sara, a young Jewish girl from his uncle's workshop, and the model Jessie Petrie who puts her hand on Mendel's leg where others would put it on his arm.

Painting a portrait frequently leads to an embrace. The artist Casimir Lypiatt exemplifies this classic artist-model confrontation when, overcome with adoration for the lovely Mrs Viveash whose portrait he paints in Huxley's *Antic Hay* of 1923, 'he put down his palette, he stepped on to the dais, he came and knelt at Mrs. Viveash's feet'.[23] At the end of a day of having his portrait painted by the woman artist Rain Carter, Demoyte, the retired headmaster of Iris Murdoch's *The Sandcastle* (1957), clasps her hand in his 'stroking it gently and conveying it frequently to his lips'.[24] Although the author accepts the convention of the artist-sitter confrontation as potentially sexual, she is unable to relinquish the convention of the male as sexual aggressor.

So strong is the model-sex link that the briefest modelling reference can carry a wealth of meaning. What else is it but sexual jealousy when in George Eliot's *Middlemarch* (1871-2) Naumann, who has painted Dorothea's portrait, discusses her beauty with Will, and Will tells him not to talk of her 'as if she were a model'.[25] Will cannot bear the thought of Dorothea's looks being a public possession, as a model was seen to belong to all men instead of being the property of one; his horror recalls Du Maurier's assertion that Trilby did not sit 'promiscuously to anybody who asked'.

The veiled sexual suggestion in the nineteenth-century's idea of modelling becomes a shorthand reference to Bohemian ways of life and love in the twentieth. Suzanne in Wyndham Lewis's *Tarr* of 1917 'had no fixed occupation. She disappeared for periods to live with men. She sat as a model.'[26] Bidlake's models in *Point Counterpoint* offered him 'facile consolations'.[27] The sexual link made modelling an easy joke which even George Bernard Shaw could not resist in act four of *The Doctor's Dilemma* (1906):

The Newspaperman	This is the studio, I suppose.
Walpole	Yes.
The Newspaperman	Where he has his models, eh?

Occasionally, posing for money is allied to greyer ways of earning a living. When Kreisler in *Tarr* considers how to make some money,

> Various pursuits presented themselves. He might go and offer himself as model at some big private studios near the Observatore. He could get a week's money advanced him. He would dress as a woman and waylay somebody or other on the boulevards. He might steal some money.[28]

The sexual stereotyping has been kept alive to the present in detective novels and thrillers in which models are always female, sexually active and dead by the end of the book.

No English authors took the sexuality implicit in modelling as far as the French, for whom posing is a metaphor for loss of virginity. In Emile Zola's *L'Oeuvre* translated into English in 1902, Claude Lantier has three days to finish his Salon picture and no model. He asks his friend Christine to make this 'supreme sacrifice' and pose nude, and she agrees.

> . . . when they stood face to face again, she ready to depart, they gazed at one another, overcome by emotion which still prevented them from speaking. Was it sadness, then, unconscious, unnameable sadness? For their eyes filled with tears, as if they had just spoilt their lives and dived to the depths of human misery. Then, moved and grieved, unable to find a word, even of thanks, he kissed her religiously upon the brow.[29]

By contrast, Claude's later seduction of Christine is a happy and trouble-free affair.

By involving their characters in modelling, nineteenth-century authors can remove them from the constricting social conventions which normally surround them. The studio scenes in Trollope's *The Last Chronicle of Barset* are remarkable for their air of intrigue. Conway Dalrymple decides to paint Clara van Siever as Jael in a picture to be executed in the silly Mrs Dobbs Broughton's boudoir. Deceit is the order of the day. Mrs Broughton decides to keep from her husband the fact that her boudoir is doubling as a studio, and Clara decides to keep the fact that she is posing a secret from her mother. Mrs Dobbs Broughton and Conway are carrying on a flirtation which neither of them feels and unknown to Clara Mrs Dobbs Broughton suggests that Conway propose to her, sure at this point that he will not. No games are equal to love-making says Trollope, 'providing that the players can be quite sure that there shall be no heart in the matter'.[30]

The details of the deceptions are unimportant. What is interesting is that the studio scenes supply the book's element of moral laxity. The picture painting episodes are a parody of the sensitivities and sensibilities of the Barsetshire relationships. The pretend passions and artifically heated feelings that go on there compare cheaply with the moral soul-searchings and fine behaviour of other couples like Major Grantly and Grace Crawley. Conway's frivolous approach to his painting is a moral point of no small importance in a society where the work ethic reigned.

The boudoir-studio in *Last Chronicle* is a secret place, an escape from the realities of life. Its picture of adult entertainment sheltering shady adult behaviour is reminiscent of the theatrical episodes in Jane Austen's *Mansfield Park* and, revealingly, the studio scenes are linked to the schemes of Madalena Demolines which Trollope calls plots and ploys. Despite the *Mansfield Park* overtones, Trollope is no Austen handing out punishments like an angel on judgement day. His interest in questions of moral behaviour is too worldly and he is too tolerant to be schematic about good and bad; ultimately he allows good to emerge from the painting episode in the form of the engagement of Clara and Conway. Even so it is interesting that Trollope, most up-to-date of authors, decides to present his scenes of shoddy behaviour in a studio, cleverly exploiting the opportunities it offers for the privacy, play-acting and hot-house sexuality which were seen as natural developments when modelling was underway.

Henry James introduces alien attitudes to the sitters' New England values while they pose for portraits in *The Europeans* of 1878. As the European-educated Felix paints Gertrude Wentworth's portrait he tells of a European life of gaiety which is utterly opposed to the life of moral duty in which her father believes. And when that father poses for his portrait a second confrontation of values takes place. Felix suggests that a flirtation with his worldly sister Eugenia might help cure Mr Wentworth's son's drink problem, an idea that so disturbs Wentworth that he refuses to pose for a fortnight. Henry James's most brilliant exploitation of the unease and excitement that surrounded the question of modelling in the nineteenth century comes in the discussion on the rights and wrongs of posing for one's portrait. Mr Wentworth's puritanical view — 'I think sitting for one's portrait is only one of the various forms of idleness' — sparks off a discussion on the subject.

'My dear sir,' said Felix, 'You can't be said to idle when you are making a man work so!'

'One might be painted while one is asleep,' suggested Mr. Brand, as a contribution to the discussion.

'Ah, do paint me while I am asleep,' said Gertrude to Felix, smiling. It had by this time become a matter of almost exciting anxiety to Charlotte what Gertrude would say or would do next.[31]

That typically Jamesian shock of the almost indecently outspoken remark in a sea of obliquity shows how modelling's sexual connotations helped authors to deal with the forbidden.

As if to stress the opposition of modelling to conventional family life, parents are frequently shown to be against it. In *The Europeans* Mr Wentworth, who is doubtful about posing, represents the puritan values of New England while his daughter, who is willing to pose, embraces the painter's values as she will before long embrace the painter. When Mrs Van Siever discovers her 25-year-old daughter decked out in her Biblical finery, the air is heavy with guilty discovered dressing up: 'Will you have the goodness to tell me miss, why you are dressed up after that Mad Bess of Bedlam fashion?'[32] Mendel's parents refer to Hetty Finch as a dirty slut and a harlot and his father tells him a cautionary tale of a sculptor who came down to carving urns for graves 'all through the drink and the models'.[33] Mrs Bagot is the mouthpiece for what is socially unacceptable about the alliance of Trilby and her son: 'If you are so *fond* of him, will you ruin him by marrying him; drag him down; prevent him from getting on in life; separate him from his sister, his family, his friends?'[34] This anti-model stance on the part of parents also explains the force of Du Maurier having Trilby's mother set her on the downward path to modelling, for modelling is in opposition to everything the family stands for.

In a variation of the bad city/good country tradition, models in fiction dwell inside, in studios, in nightclubs and, in the case of Miriam's model, in the catacombs of Rome. After Trilby has renounced Little Billee and begun her purgatorial journey to innocence she goes to the country. And whereas Mendel's scenes with his model-mistresses

Sara, Hetty and Jessie take place indoors, many of the scenes with Morrison, his one true love, take place on Hampstead Heath.

The picture-slashing episode is modelling's great set-piece, comparable to the never-darken-my-doors-again scene of nineteenth-century melodrama and the discovery-of-adultery scene in the contemporary novel. Trollope has a picture-slashing episode in *Last Chronicle*. While not so heavily dramatic as some — the author tells us that the canvas was later patched and exhibited — it is clear that to get Clara and Conway out of their boudoir-studio world of deception and into the daylight, the canvas has to be slit in four.

Anger at the artist or jealousy of the person depicted are the most common motives for picture slashing. The model Bessie destroys Dick Heldar's painting of *Melancholia* in Rudyard Kipling's *The Light That Failed* of 1891, to spite the artist for spoiling her romance with the war correspondent Torpenhow.

> Bessie faithfully tidied up the studio, set the door ajar for flight, emptied half a bottle of turpentine on a duster, and began to scrub the face of the Melancholia viciously. The paint did not smudge quickly enough. She took a palette-knife and scraped, following each stroke with the wet duster. In five minutes the picture was a formless, scarred muddle of colours.[35]

A feared rival is the subject of the portrait slashed in Mrs Humphrey Ward's *Fenwick's Career*, which had its first of many printings in 1906. John Fenwick pursues his painting career in London, keeping quiet about his wife Phoebe in Westmorland. He is taken up by Lord Findon and his unhappily married daughter Eugenie de Pastourelles, whose portrait he paints and manages to sell. Elated by his success, he sets a sketch for the portrait on the easel, lights a lamp on either side of it, and goes off to Peter Robinson to buy Phoebe a present. Meanwhile Phoebe hears that John is passing as an unmarried man in London. She comes to his studio and is confronted by the altar-like portrait:

> With dry, reddened eyes, she stared at the portrait of the

woman who must have stolen John from her . . . She caught up a large brush, dipped it in the paint and going to the picture — panting and crimson — she daubed it from top to bottom, blotting out the eyes, the mouth, the beautiful outline of the head, — above all, the hands, whose delicate whiteness especially enraged her.[36]

In Somerset Maugham's *The Moon and Sixpence* (1918) Dirk Stroeve finds a nude painting of his dead wife Blanche in the studio of Charles Strickland, the painter she had left him for:

It was the picture of a woman lying on a sofa, with one arm beneath her head and the other along her body; one knee was raised and the other leg was stretched out. The pose was classic. Stroeve's head swam. It was Blanche. Grief and jealousy and rage seized him and he cried out hoarsely; he was inarticulate; he clenched his fists and raised them threateningly at an invisible enemy. He screamed at the top of his voice. He was beside himself. He could not bear it. That was too much. He looked round wildly for some instrument; he wanted to hack the picture to pieces; it should not exist another minute . . . At last he came upon what he sought, a large scraper, and he pounced on it with a cry of triumph. He seized it as though it were a dagger, and ran to the picture . . .[37]

He does not make the hole he intended: 'It was a work of art. I couldn't touch it. I was afraid.' The threatened portrait in Oscar Wilde's *The Picture of Dorian Gray* (1891) also remains intact, but the threat to mutilate is as strong a shock to readers' systems as the act of mutilation. As the artist attempts to rip it up, Dorian cries

'Don't, Basil, don't,' . . . 'It would be murder.'
'I am glad you appreciate my work at last, Dorian,' said the painter, coldly, when he had recovered from his surprise. 'I never thought you could.'
'Appreciate it? I am in love with it, Basil. It is a part of myself. I feel that.'[38]

The power of such scenes comes from the feeling that it is a person and not an object that is being destroyed. Ideas of images that *are* the person they embody are probably as old as art. The classical writers record several tales of humans falling in love with statues. Pliny tells of the man who fell in love with Praxiteles' Cnidian Venus and 'concealing himself in the temple during the night, gratified his lustful passion upon it, traces of which are to be seen in a stain left upon the marble'.[39] Athenaeus tells of Clisophus who fell in love with a statue 'and shut himself up in the temple to gratify his affection'.[40] Vasari supplies a Renaissance link with the story of Fra Bartolommeo's beautiful nude Saint Sebastian:

> It is said that while this figure was on exhibition in the church the friars found out by the confessional that women had sinned in regarding it, owing to the realistic skill of Fr. Bartolommeo; accordingly they removed it and put it in the chapter house.[41]

Fiction comes at the end of the line of love-inspiring images. One of the oddest versions is Thomas Hardy's short story 'Barbara of the House of Grebe'. Barbara, daughter of Sir John and Lady Grebe, elopes with Edmund Willowes. Edmund goes to Europe where he poses for a marble bust. In Venice, he is disfigured in a fire, and on his return Barbara, horrified by his appearance, cannot live with him. He goes away and is presumed dead. Barbara marries Lord Uplandtowers whom she does not love. One day the full-size sculpture of her first husband arrives. She places it in her boudoir and visits it at night. Lord Uplandtowers follows her: 'Arrived at the door of her boudoir, he beheld the door of the private recess open, and Barbara within it, standing with her arms clasped tightly round the neck of her Edmund, and her mouth on his.'[42] Lord Uplandtowers has the statue disfigured, as Willowes was disfigured, and puts it in a wardrobe at the end of the marriage bed. The next night he pulls a cord, the doors open and Barbara is confronted with the hideously disfigured statue of her first husband. She has an epileptic fit and develops a passionate sexual interest in Lord Uplandtowers bearing him eleven children in nine years.

A late Victorian refinement on this theme is the work of

art that takes on life. This was expressed at its most popular level in the living statues music-hall turn in which actors and actresses painted themselves white and posed like sculptures. And in its most macabre form it is shown in Dorian Gray's portrait developing the wrinkles he avoids or the model in Edgar Allan Poe's *The Oval Portrait* dying as the artist puts the finishing touch to her likeness. In paint, treatment of the Pygmalion and Galatea myth abounded and in Fred Anstey's comic tale of 1885, *Tinted Venus*, a nude statue moves into the home of a man who has placed a ring on her finger.

In *The Marble Aphrodite* by Anthony Kirby Gill (1912) the sculptor Aubrey Carroll falls in love with a naiad who emerges from his garden pond. She models for a statue of Aphrodite which is so beautiful he decides to destroy it for fear it will stop him loving the naiad:

> Approaching his Aphrodite, he placed the sharp point of the chisel close to her face, and raising his arm, prepared to deal the blow that would destroy its divine beauty for ever. But in that one instant her eyes, heavy, as it seemed, with the languor of dreams, encountered his own, and his arms dropped powerless to his sides.[43]

This is a strongly anti-woman book. In falling in love with the statue whose perfection 'nature could never, in any circumstances, attain to', he has denied two women: the married Lady Vidal whose offer of love he rebuffs and the naiad whom he abandons. It is tempting to see this fascination with living statues in terms of art as the extreme form of the nineteenth-century's mimetic aesthetic and, in terms of life, as the extreme form of the nineteenth-century's attitude to sex, the fantasy of a sculptured love object untainted by the sounds and smells of a real woman.

Missing from all the above depictions of the female model is an exploration of her point of view. *Alberta and Freedom* (1931), the second novel in the Norwegian Cora Sandel's trilogy, opens with the heroine Alberta modelling for an Englishman in turn of the century Paris, a job she does solely for the freedom the money buys her. Alberta in front of a stranger to the studio feels unprotected:

Tensely, a little convulsively she would stand enduring the stranger's gaze, racked by defiance and antipathy. She understood the model who once, at Colarossi's, suddenly pulled a face at someone who had come in and just stood and stared. She understood the prostitute who hurls a contemptuous term of abuse in the face of the woman walking by. She felt an obscure solidarity with them.[44]

The book's professional model, Alphonsine, 'was no longer young, but she was a sought-after model, because she was perceptive, punctual, and without caprice'. She warns Alberta against sitting without pay to her friend Sivert:

A fellow like that needs you, I can see that. But when you are worn out with standing for him and sitting for him, going hungry and cold with him and perhaps submitting your self to all sorts of things for his and his art's sake, he will become successful one day, and then you can pack your bags.[45]

In 1963, Margaret Drabble, chronicler of the lot of the middle-class Englishwoman, shows that she too had considered the face of modelling behind the stereotype. Explaining the break-up of her marriage to Tony in *A Summer Birdcage*, Gill says:

We used to quarrel about such stupid things like money and food . . . and then he was painting all the time and he seemed to think that I ought to be happy just sitting around in the nude and letting him paint me, and cooking him the odd meal. And it got so bloody cold, posing, especially when they cut the electricity off and the fire wouldn't work. Oh it was awful. I wanted to do things too. I didn't like just waiting on him. I kept saying, 'You could pay someone to do that.'[46]

The cold, discomfort and embarrassment do not appear in the stereotyped accounts, which are not concerned with how it feels to be a model. The low-key and convincing picture of modelling in these last two books, along with the description of Miss Churm's satisfactions in James's *The Real Thing*, is the voice of reality in the midst of wishful or lazy thinking.

Notes

1 Oscar Wilde, 'The Model Millionaire', *World*, 22 June 1887, reprinted in *Lord Arthur Savile's Crime and Other Stories* (London, 1891).

2 Nathaniel Hawthorne, *The Marble Faun* (Ohio, 1968), ch. 4.

3 Michael Innes, 'The Flight of Patroclus', *Appleby Talking* (Gollancz, 1954), pp. 57-62.

4 Arnold Bennett, 'The Artist's Model', *Titbits*, 6 May 1893.

5 Sir Edward Bulwer-Lytton, *Lucretia or The Children of Night* (London, 1846), ch. 10.

6 Ibid., ch. 2.

7 Richard Jenkyns, *The Victorians and Ancient Greece* (Blackwell, 1980), ch. 7.

8 James Stanley Little, *Whose Wife Shall She Be?* (London, 1888), p. 285.

9 George Du Maurier, *Trilby*, 1894 (Dent, 1956), part 2, pp. 76-7.

10 Ibid., part 8, p. 323.

11 Ibid., part 3, p. 94.

12 Ibid., p. 97.

13 Ibid., p. 97.

14 Gilbert Cannan, *Mendel* (London, 1916), Book 1, ch. 9.

15 Ibid.

16 Ibid., p. 129.

17 William de Morgan, *Alice-For-Short* (London, 1907), ch. 17.

18 Margery Allingham, *Death of a Ghost*, 1934, (Heinemann, 1964), p. 33.

19 Ibid., p. 32.

20 Ibid., p. 35.

21 Aldous Huxley, *Point Counterpoint*, 1928 (Panther, 1978), ch. 4.

22 Anthony Powell, *At Lady Molly's*, 1957 (Fontana, 1980), p. 134.

23 Aldous Huxley, *Antic Hay* (London, 1923), ch. 6.

24 Iris Murdoch, *The Sandcastle* (London, Chatto & Windus, 1957), p. 107.

25 George Eliot, *Middlemarch* (Pan, 1973), ch. 22.

26 P. Wyndham Lewis, *Tarr* (London, 1918), part II, ch. 1.

27 Huxley, *Point Counterpoint*, ch. 11.

28 Lewis, *Tarr*, part 2, ch. 8.

29 Emile Zola, *His Masterpiece* (London, Vizetelly, 1902), ch. 4.

30 Anthony Trollope, *The Last Chronicle of Barset* (London, 1867) 'The Picture'.

31 Henry James, *The Europeans* (London, 1878), ch. 5.

32 Trollope, *Last Chronicle*, 'The End of Jael and Sisera'.

33 Cannan, *Mendel*, Book 1, p. 80.

34 Du Maurier, *Trilby*, Part 4, p. 148.
35 Rudyard Kipling, *The Light That Failed* (London, 1890), ch. 9.
36 Mrs Humphrey Ward, *Fenwick's Career* (London, 1906), ch. 8.
37 W. Somerset Maugham, *The Moon and Sixpence*, 1919 (Pan, 1980), ch. 39.
38 Oscar Wilde, *The Picture of Dorian Gray*, 1891 (Oxford University Press, 1974), p. 27.
39 Pliny, *Natural History*, Book 36, ch. 4.
40 Athenaeus, Book 13, ch. 84.
41 Vasari, *Lives*, vol. 2, p. 196.
42 Thomas Hardy, 'Barbara of the House of Grebe', *The Short Stories of Thomas Hardy* (London, Macmillan, 1928), p. 564.
43 Anthony Kirby Gill, *The Marble Aphrodite* (London, 1912), ch. 16.
44 Cora Sandel, *Alberta and Freedom*, 1931 (The Women's Press, 1980), p. 8.
45 Ibid., p. 101.
46 Margaret Drabble, *A Summer Birdcage*, 1963 (Penguin, 1975), p. 39.

10
The Model in Art

The scrubbiest tree and lowliest peasant have had more attention paid them as subjects of painting than have artists' models. Scholars have shown how in order to improve his compositions Constable shifted bits of East Anglia about like so many stage props. The sketch books of the German Romantic painter Casper David Friedrich reveal how he used the same few motifs, composing them to make points about the existence of God in nature. The interest of early nineteenth-century landscapists in catching the reality of clouds in the sky instead of keeping to the stylized cloud shapes that had done for centuries, has been used as evidence that the period's religious and scientific theories were affecting art. The depiction of English labourers has revealed the beliefs of the governing classes who commissioned the paintings. Yet the various appearances in post-Renaissance painting of the artist's model have been ignored.

The earliest representations of models in paintings are religious illustrations of the legend of St Luke drawing the Virgin. This theme, of which Rogier van der Weyden's version in the Museum of Fine Arts, Boston, is the best known, was a speciality of Dutch fifteenth and sixteenth-century artists. By the seventeenth century, the Dutch had secularized the subject, and were producing scenes of the artist in the studio at work before the model. Often, as in Vermeer's *A Painter in His Studio*, the model is clothed, in this case as the muse Clio, but in Michael Sweerts' *Drawing Academy* in the Frans Halsmuseum, the artists draw a fine-bodied male model. Female life models were used in seventeenth-century Holland, but their second-rate status in the context of Renaissance theory, and the aura of sexuality

160

which surrounded them made them unfit for perpetuation in the superior medium of oil. Female models who were recorded were done so in the more informal and less important medium of pen or pencil (fig. 1). Engravings of artists working from casts, in Baccio Bandinelli's academies show that by the sixteenth century the Italians were also producing pictures of artists at work, and in the seventeenth century this theme was taken up by the French. Isolated paintings of model subjects from the classical writers in the sixteenth and seventeenth centuries gathered strength in the eighteenth, with Zeuxis and the five maidens particularly popular, though Apelles and Campaspe were also painted. Female life class models began to be shown in the studio interiors frequently painted in the neo-classical era. Auguste-Antoine Masse showed a nude woman modelling in his *L'Atelier des elèves de Gros a l'institut*, 1824 (Musée Marmotton, Paris).

In eighteenth-century France a new category of titillating artist and model paintings in contemporary dress was born; Fragonard's *The New Model* (fig. 19) shows an artist using his mahlstick to raise the hem of a prospective model's skirt. In nineteenth-century England the Dutch studio pictures emerged in Victorian form in W.P. Frith's *The Sleepy Model* (fig. 21) and the erotic approach of the French surfaced as the century drew to a close in smoking-room pictures like Frank Hyde's pair of paintings called *A Visit To The Studo*.[1] In the first painting, the schoolboy peeps behind the screen at the forbidden nude model; in the second he sips wine with her. All over Europe, the Pygmalion myth was added to the classical subject canon and Vasari replaced the classical writers as a source of model anecdote: Ingres in the nineteenth century and Picasso in this both painted Raphael and his mistress model.

All paintings with models reveal something of the attitudes of the age in which they were painted, though not all to the same degree. Most straightforward are the *académies*, transcriptions of models posing, done to show the artists' skill in painting from life. In his self-portrait in the Louvre, L.E. Melendez (or Menendez, 1716-80) displays with great pride his *académie* of the back of a male model. These *académies* are portraits of models — or would be if the sitters were not anonymous — and show the poses that were fashionable and the type of body that was admired at the time of painting.

Until the practice died out in the middle of this century, every student of fine art had to produce them as evidence of skill. Paintings of studio scenes, the other manifestation of the factual treatment of the artist's model, have never declined, as can be seen by a glance round any art school graduation show.

Some model paintings say as much about the parent genres which inspired them as about the model. Vermeer's *Painter in His Studio* has more in common with quiet Dutch seventeenth-century scenes of the middle classes about their tasks than it does with an informative life class picture like the one by Sweerts. Fragonard's artist-model confrontation fits into a broader eighteenth-century category of erotic pictures typified by another of Fragonard's works, *The Swing*, in the Wallace Collection. But messages about the models can still be heard. Models are not painted as muses (or muses as models) unless it is wished to state their importance to the painter. And a model could not be shown in a sexual situation unless it were felt to be convincing. Fragonard's *The New Model* reveals a lot about eighteenth-century attitudes to the model: the equation of model with prostitute is made clear by the second woman who has unveiled the model's breasts to the artist and stands like a procuress while he inspects the young girl's ankles.

Model paintings can be a way to show the artist's allegiance to a set of aesthetic ideas. Given that an age reveals itself in the myths it finds appealing, the frequent choice of Zeuxis and the five models that marks the neo-classical period has much to say about artists' attitudes in the second half of the eighteenth century. Those who used it, like Angelika Kauffmann and J.L. Vincent, wished to upgrade their status by pointing to the similarity between their own practice of drawing from models and that of the classical world. By selecting a subject which shows a reknowned classical painter exercising his power of selection, the artists were painting a classical precedent for the practice of their own age which also believed in an aesthetic of the ideal.

Evidence of artistic belief does not have to be as self-conscious as neo-classicism's choice of suitable subjects from the classics. More than an amusing subject with a guaranteed appeal to a Victorian audience, Frith's *The Sleepy Model* (fig. 21) is a document which reveals the way in which the nineteenth-century academic artists saw themselves suffering good-humouredly at the hands of the models on whom they depended. The model was an orange-seller Frith had taken to his studio in order to paint her bewitching smile, a smile which refused to appear at the artist's command:

> After many attempts to raise an expression that would help me to make a laughing face, I found the worst of hindrances that can affect a painter come upon me — my model fell fast asleep; and as nothing that I could say or do would keep her awake, I abandoned the laughing subject and painted 'The Sleepy Model', who now sleeps all day long in the Diploma Gallery. By showing a laughing face sketched on the canvas before which a perplexed artist stands, and the model, who ought to assist him in realising in the expression, fast asleep, I thought I should prove in a small way one of the difficulties that beset all artists — to say nothing of the situation which has its comic side.[2]

Certain model paintings reveal a great deal about their age through the depiction of the model. In Mariano Fortuny y Marsal's late nineteenth-century painting *The Choice of a Model* (Corcoran Gallery, Washington) a group of men appraise a model who stands naked on a piano. Although clearly designed as a voyeuristic fantasy, the artist has avoided implicating his nineteenth-century audience in seeming to stare at the model by clothing the surrogate spectators within the frame in eighteenth-century costume. The woman wears nothing at all, although a pile of her recently removed clothes lies on the floor by the piano.

The sex of the model depends on the type of painting. The majority of factual works, the *académies*, and until 150 years ago the studio pictures, show male models. But when the documentary approach is abandoned, and in nearly all paintings of the last hundred years, the models become female. Women models are nearly always accompanied by a pile of discarded clothes, rather as St Peter always carries a key in Renaissance paintings and Saint Jerome always has a lion nearby. It is their sign. The just-removed clothes draw attention to the act of undressing which has led to the model's naked state, thereby presenting two titillating ideas in one picture.

Despite the variety, one of the things pictures of female models have in common, the factual as well as the fanciful, the fifteenth century as well as the nineteenth, is that in all of them the model is passive. The model is the object of the gaze not just of the artist within the picture but of those outside the painting as well.

Until the mid nineteenth century, the normal presentation of models in paintings was as anonymous figures to be stared at unobstructed and unabashed. All model paintings had an element of voyeurism built into them. The artist in the gilt frame stares at the model and the gallery visitors outside it stare at her too. Then in 1855 a painting appeared which subverted that expectation by presenting the model as active. Courbet's *The Painter's Studio* (fig. 22) marks the new model's introduction as she stands looking over the artist's shoulder at the work he is doing. *The Painter's Studio* was followed by others. In France there were Manet's *L'Olympia* (fig. 23) shown at the 1865 salon and *Déjeuner sur l'herbe*, 1863 (fig. 24) and Seurat's *Les Poseuses* of 1888 (fig. 27); in England, Whistler's two sketches of 1866-7 for the projected *Artist in the Studio* (fig. 20); in America, Thomas Eakins's *William Rush and his Model* of 1908 (fig. 18); in Germany, Kirchner's 1907 *Self-Portrait With Model* (fig. 25) and Schmidt-Rottluff's *Rest in the Studio*, 1910 (Künsthalle, Hamburg). All of them show that this new non-passive model appeared in the work of several artists in various countries up to the outbreak of the First World War.

The painters who followed Courbet baffled the possibility of voyeurism by subverting the conventional ways of depicting the model. One method used was to have the models in the paintings return the spectators' gaze, catching them at the keyhole as it were. Although in neither of Manet's paintings is the woman represented as a model, she was known at the time to be one. In fact, public knowledge of her identity was a factor in the notoriety of *L'Olympia* and *Déjeuner sur l'herbe*. Yet this woman whose role it is to be stared at, stares back out at us, intercepting the spectators gaze and making herself a force to be reckoned with rather than a characterless nude to be stared at uninterrupted. A variation appears in the Kirchner *Self-Portrait with Model*. Although the model seems unaware of our gaze as she sits on the bed, she is protected by the belligerent presence of the painter as he stares out of the canvas into spectator space.

A second method was not to have the model do the one thing models are supposed to do, and that is pose. Though thousands of words have gone into breaking the code of Courbet's proclamation of his artistic and social beliefs in *The Painter's Studio*, no definitive meaning of his painting exists. But one thing leaps out at even the most unsophisticated observer and that is that the model is pictured outside her normal role. Although her nakedness makes her profession explicit, she is not practising it. Instead of standing in front of the artist's eyes, she looks over his shoulder at the painting on which he is working. Placed on the artist's side of the easel, she must be one of the earliest models in art not being looked at by the characters in the painting but doing the looking herself. Kirchner's model also refuses to meet the viewer's expectations. She keeps on some of her clothes, she sits on the bed instead of posing and she stays on the artist's side of the easel. The model in Eakins's *William Rush and His Model* does not pose either. She has finished working, and as she is helped down from the model's throne by the sculptor, she moves — the model's cardinal sin.

A third way to emphasize the model's lack of passivity was to make her important, and the simplest way to do this was to give her a dominant place in the picture. In Courbet's *The Artist's Studio* she is part of the central group of artist, child and dog, while everyone else is crowded into the wings of the painting. Seurat emphasizes that it is the three models who are the subject of his picture by giving them a central position within the composition and naming his picture after them. Because in Eakins's painting the model is higher than the painter who helps her down from the dais, the impression is that of a courtier handing down a queen.

All the paintings which subvert the traditional way of viewing the model are manifesto paintings, paintings in which the artists are trying to state something important about their beliefs. What are they saying, and why did they use the model to help them say it?

Much of the power of Manet's *L'Olympia* stems from the courtesan's composed presence and individuality. Far from being a French Salon nude — that is, a nineteenth-century equivalent of a pin-up girl — she has a definite face and a specific body. Manet's depiction of a strongly individualized woman is an attack on the high-art Barbie dolls that passed for nudes in academic circles. The fact that the name of the model has come down to us along with the picture suggests it was part of Manet's strategy to stress that a particular model posed for the image. Through her he is displaying his radical artistic beliefs.

Whistler's two small sketches, *The Artist's Studio* and *Whistler in his Studio*, both done as preparation for a projected but never painted major work of ten by six feet for the 1866 Salon, are also manifesto works. The desire to scandalize the conservatives was a major element in its conception. On 15 August 1865, Whistler wrote to Fantin-Latour,

> Il y a toi et Moore, le fille blanche assise sur un canapé, at la Japonaise que se promene! enfin un apothéose de tout ce qui peut scandaliser les Academicians, les couleurs choisies sont charmantes. Moi en gris clair — la robe blanche de Jo — la robe couleur de chair de la Japonaise (vue de dos) toi et Moore en noir — le fond de l'atelier gris . . .[3]

Though it is not clear whether it is the muted colour scheme, a symphony in black, pale grey, white and flesh, that would scandalize the academicians, or the characters, the models Jo Hiffernan and the Japanese woman and the artists, Whistler himself, Albert Moore and Fantin Latour who would horrify them, this painting reveals a lot about Whistler's attitude to art in the mid-1860s. After a period of producing paintings influenced by the classicizing anti-anecdotal works of Albert Moore whom he met in 1865, paintings of women dressed in white, paintings influenced by Japanese prints and increasingly more simplified sea and river scapes, a lull was setting in, related to his indecision as to what to do next. He seems to be taking stock in the projected painting; all the influences and achievements to date are represented through the models, the artists and the colour scheme. Clearly the decision of where to go next was too hard to take at this time, which is why the projected painting was never produced, why he broke off his London painting career for his mysterious visit to Valparaiso in 1866, why his stream of important finished paintings dried up until 1871 and the portrait of his mother.

Seurat's *Les Poseuses* is definitely a manifesto painting of some kind, since the artist has put an earlier major work, *A Sunday Afternoon on the Island of Grande Jatte*, 1884-6, against the studio wall behind the three models. None of the explanations of this work accounts for the models, let alone their prominent position. But given the lead of the school of commentators who make much of Seurat's attempts to elevate the lowly by making history pictures of their everyday existence, as in *Une Baignade*, 1884, with its distant factory chimneys and workmen resting on the bank of the Seine, or the *Grande Jatte* with its lower-middle-class Parisians enjoying Sunday on the island in the Seine, it seems reasonable to assume that some reasssessment of the position and importance of the female model is being offered by the painter. It may be significant that the head of the seated model on the left almost eclipses the monkey the woman is walking on a lead in the *Grande Jatte*. Monkeys were a traditional symbol of lasciviousness so he could be making a point about the unjust slurs of immorality slung at professional models.

Thomas Eakins's *William Rush and His Model* pays an extraordinary homage to the model. Rush was an early American sculptor who persuaded a young and chaperoned Philadelphian to model nude for an allegorical figure he was carving for the city's waterworks. Eakins was fascinated by Rush, and produced three other versions of the subject showing the girl posing for the sculptor. But they were traditional treatments of Rush working from the model: only this one shows Rush treating the model like a queen. Lloyd Goodrich in an Eakins exhibition catalogue of 1961 says that Eakins occasionally asked women sitting for portraits if they would pose for him nude, and this together with Rush's resemblance to Eakins in the portrait, suggests that Eakins identified with Rush.[4] But the painting shows something even stronger was at work. Eakins believed that knowledge of the figure was the basis of artistic skill, and yet he could see the confused attitudes that surrounded the nude model in the late nineteenth century: a drawing done while a student at the Pennsylvania Academy of the Fine Arts of a nude model in the face mask protocol demanded she wear is testimony to this. Later hating the hypocrisy surrounding the model in the prudish Philadelphia of the 1880s, he removed the loincloth from a male model at a women's class he was teaching at the Pennsylvania Academy. *William Rush and His Model* is a manifesto work because to show an artist handing a model down from the dias is a revolutionary act at a time when models wore masks as a kind of purdah and loincloths as a badge of their shameful sexuality, and yet drawing from life was taught as the basis of a fine art education.

In his *Self-Portrait with Model* Kirchner is telling the world he is an artist not a gentleman. To advertise that the rules of the academic artists and their bourgeois clients have nothing to do with him, he defiantly puts his model by his side. At the period of the painting Kirchner was a member of *Die Brücke*, a group of German artists who led a Bohemian life as part of their avant-garde artistic beliefs. Recalling this time in middle age, he said that he never again found such beautiful and understanding models as those at Dresden: 'one did not only paint them, but discussed and read aloud with them Strindberg, Ibsen, Wedekind, Maupassant and much poetry'.[5] It is this self-contained world of artists and models which is pictured in the self-portrait. Kirchner is larger and to the front of the model, but both are in a similar state of undress, she in her underwear, he in a blue and orange striped robe beneath which he is naked. It is a depiction of Bohemianism, the artist's statement that the pictures he paints are inseparable from the life he lives.

There is nothing new about manifesto paintings. Though Courbet needed 16 by 13 feet to contain all the characters necessary to express his political, social and artistic beliefs, he is only doing what Reynolds did when he painted himself standing next to a bust of Michelangelo in order to proclaim his belief in his predecessor's greatness, his association with Michelangelo's approach to his work and his view of himself as an aspiring successor. By confronting the public with his model and himself in an equal state of undress in their private Bohemian world, Kirchner is acting no more outrageously than Hogarth when he pictured himself minus his wig and with inelegantly sprawled legs as he sketched the comic muse on his canvas, puncturing in one image what he saw as the pretentiousness of eighteenth-century art and artists. What is new is not the painting as manifesto but the choice of the model through which to make the statements. How did the model become such a powerful image at this period?

Certain statements only have the power to shock at certain times and it seems that the model shown in a situation of importance or of equality with the artist had an extremely strong shock value in the years between 1850 and 1920. The reason for this lies in the view of respectable womanhood held at this time. In the nineteenth century, the most admired type of female was distinguished by a cluster of characteristics which included purity, modesty, duty and self-sacrifice. These characteristics were enhanced like jewels by a domestic setting. A correlation was made between women's ignorance and their innocence. It was women's lack of contact with the values of the male world which allowed their particular group of virtues to develop. Home was where the woman reigned and where she could influence her children and harbour her husband from the storms of the masculine world that raged outside. This profile of the middle-class woman of the second half of the nineteenth century, give or take a few differences or changes in emphasis — the French stress on marriage for the advancement of status and fortunes, the English stress on true love within marriage inspired by the example of Victoria and Albert — was common to most advanced Western countries.

The cult of the woman as the angel in the house (Coventry Patmore published a series of poems under this title in the mid 1850s) which was the officially approved face of Victorian womanhood, ensured that the depiction of women in any other guise would draw a vast amount of attention. A woman naked and unashamed in a studio, not passively suffering her horrible fate but apparently at ease in her role and her surroundings, would have been a difficult image for the nineteenth-century viewer to cope with. A quick leaf through the model images imprinted on their minds would not help them in the face of models returning the spectators' stares, a model treated like a queen, or a model placed in the centre of a painting while big names like Baudelaire were relegated to its edges.

Most conventional gallery-goers in the nineteenth century saw the female model as necessary to the production of art but with certain troubling areas of immorality and low status which were confusing to consider in connection with paintings and sculptures. Because it was not nineteenth-century conventional wisdom to see the model on an equal footing with the artist or the viewer, Courbet and Co. were assured of attention. Just as blasphemy has most power to shock in a religious age, these painters realized that to elevate the artist's model on to a rung of equality with the artist and to paint her in an active and not a passive role had most force in an age which felt the model was better kept out of sight.

It is no coincidence that Murger's tales of Bohemian life preceded the first of these paintings by only a few years. Fortified by the publicizing of Bohemia as a society different from but parallel to conventional society, artists began to put it on to their canvases, equating for the first time in history their advanced ideas about art with their advanced ideas about life. The conventional Frith's irritation and amusement at his sleepy model has only to be compared with the avant-garde Whistler's decision to place his models at the artist's side in his projected Salon painting, to appreciate the revolutionary way in which these artists saw their models.

It would be absurd to claim that all model pictures at this period are manifesto works. Young artists continued to paint studio interiors, like the *Studio of Gustave Moreau* done by his pupil Matisse in 1895, because studios were where young artists worked and it was inexpensive and convenient to paint their surroundings. The two paintings by Matisse and Marquet of each other painting nude female models in 1904-5 are friendship pictures, works of art which cement the shared ideals and comradeship from which Fauvism was to emerge; but a bowl of fruit could replace the model without losing the point of the paintings.

By 1920 the days of the model-manifesto painting were over. Bohemianism had given models the right to be seen at the artist's side and though the public might not approve it had to accept. The model sailed serenely into twentieth-century paintings where, nude and female, she marked a new entry in the dictionary of subject matter, a category like landscape or still life. She has ancestors in the *académies*, but the twentieth-century difference is that now she is called *The Model* and not *Une Académie*; she is a subject in her own right and not a studio exercise to show the painter's skill. When Harold Gilman paints *The Model* in 1911 it is what it says it is. It differs from its ancestors in showing neither the artist at work before the model nor an anecdotal view of the model, but a model plain and simple, a new twentieth-century subject. Matthew Smith did several paintings of models between the wars with titles such as *Model Turning*, and not as they would have been once, *Reclining Nude* or *Sleeping Venus*. By this acknowledgment, the model is rescued from the anonymity of earlier centuries.

This century has seen other incarnations of the model. Picasso uses her to explore his obsessions with sexuality, ageing, beauty and impotence in the etchings of the 1960s and 1970s. Philip Pearlstein, the American artist at the centre of a group of New Realist painters, has done several paintings of professional models. A typical one, *Model Standing by Easel*, 1974 (fig. 26) is just that, an honest look at a lumpy, bumpy, studio model with her elbow on the back of the easel. The feminist painters, painters that is who share a belief, whatever its variations, that women have been and still are handicapped in this society, have examined models too. Through their awareness that artist's 'model' has come to mean a women as an object eyed by a man, they have begun to question the role and the presentation of the model in art. Some, fearful of repeating the old and prejudiced ways of seeing, think hard before they commit their images of men to canvas. Others question the division of art implicit in the model into painter (male) and model (female).

Looked at across countries and centuries, the paintings give a complete picture of modelling. The points made in the preceding chapters can be found within the picture frames: the importance of the male model in teaching students how to draw; the connection of female models with sex; the change in the attitude towards the model brought by Bohemia; her existence in this century as a subject in her own right; the feminists' questioning of the attitudes that lie behind the constant presentation of the model as female.

Silently the paintings have recorded them all.

Notes

1 Illustrated in Mark Girouard, *Life in the English Country House*, 1978 (Penguin, 1980) p. 297.
2 Frith, *My Autobiography*, vol. 1, p. 249.
3 McLaren Young, *Whistler*, text vol., p. 37.
4 *Thomas Eakins* (Smithsonian Institution, 1961), pp. 19-20.
5 W. Grohmann, *E.L. Kirchner* (Thames and Hudson, 1962), p. 38.

Index